GH00786566

The Business Dime

how to be successful in managin

ABOUT THE AUTHORS

Sandra Stephens

Sandra Stephens is 46 years old with 2 grown children, Robert and Jill. She lives and works in Sheffield. She currently works for the Facilities Directorate at Sheffield Hallam University, and was instrumental in the introduction of the department's business planning process.

Prior to joining the university, Sandra worked for the Department for Employment in Sheffield and was part of the team responsible for initiating the Government's Lifelong Learning Initiative.

Sandra sees herself as an advocate of that initiative, having embarked and achieved an MBA after her fortieth birthday.

Margaret Dale

Margaret Dale is a Human Resources Consultant who has written extensively in the area of people management. She is the author of *The People Dimension* (Blackhall Publishing).

The Business Dimension
how to be successful in managing your business

Sandra Stephens
with Margaret Dale

BLACKHALL
Publishing

This book was typeset by Red Dot for

BLACKHALL PUBLISHING
26 Eustace Street
Dublin 2
Ireland

e-mail: blackhall@tinet.ie

© Sandra Stephens, 1999

ISBN: 1 901657 58 2

Printed in Ireland by
Betaprint Ltd

CONTENTS

With all my love to my family,
particularly
Robert and Jill

INTRODUCTION

This book focuses on the whys and hows of measuring success in the business world. No attempt is made to examine the academic and theoretical concepts emphasised by business schools and management consultants. Instead, it is intended to provide the reader with a common-sense approach to planning systems that help underpin successful business development. This book is written in such a way as to stimulate basic awareness of the need for planning and the need to measure goals when pursuing operational success. It takes a step by step approach to what this author believes are the first questions that budding business people might ask as they take their first steps up the ladder of the commercial world.

Initially, we look at why there is a need to plan for success. This may sound rather strange, as some may think that success is the result of good luck and good judgement rather than a result of well-planned objectives. This book argues to the contrary, placing great importance on the need for effective planning at all stages of the business and its operations.

Every aspect of the business needs to be fully understood if success is to be had, although some may argue that that may be a 'belt and braces' approach to commerce. Yet how can an organisation or business say that it is successful unless it can *prove* that it is successful, and not only to its shareholders, but to the workforce and even to its customers?

Some thought is also given as to how to create a business plan. This part of the book is intended to show the importance of a non-financial business plan, focusing on the strategic and operational aspects that play integral parts in business development. It does *not* look at the financial business plan per se, mainly because, in the opinion of this author, too much emphasis is placed on the 'bottom line' and the number crunching activities within an organisation. This book hopes to address this imbalance and looks at the need to measure success through non-financial functions, and to look at a more humanist approach to successful business.

Without an effective and informed workforce, today's businesses will struggle to achieve or maintain success. It is vitally important that organisations recognise the need for encouraging individuals within the workforce to believe in the organisation, allow them to play a supportive role and make sure they understand the implications of their efforts on overall visions and goals. However, recognising that importance and being able to do something about it requires a real commitment from everyone in the organisation.

Maintaining a balanced approach is strived for throughout this book, which questions the need for measuring for success. It is not enough to be able to say 'yes, we as an organisation are very successful', and then hope that everyone believes you. Crossing one's fingers is never enough! Shareholders, stakeholders, the workforce, and customers need to know if the business is successful, and not only *if* it is, but *how* it is successful. To be able to measure success takes an awful lot of effort if it is to be done effectively.

Successful organisations need to be able to point to the areas *where* they are successful, and they need to be able to recognise those areas that are not successful or need improving. Business systems need to be developed to be able to do that. Effective business tools need to be established to make the process of measurement more useful and more user-friendly. This book hopes to provide some help in that area.

To conclude this introduction and to sum up the overall aim of this book, two questions spring to mind:

'How well is the business doing today?'
'Show me how successful our business is.'

If those questions prove difficult, you need some help to develop and establish systems and procedures that will provide answers to those asking the questions. Hopefully, you will find the help you need in the chapters that follow.

1

WHY PLAN?

Key learning points from this chapter are:
- Why there is a need to plan for business success.
- How to identify achievable business goals.
- How to anticipate obstacles that might block those goals.
- Why it is important to fully understand the business environment.
- Understanding why it is important to be able to measure success.

1.1 INTRODUCTION

Writers are often told 'only write about what you know'. Perhaps the same can be said about running or managing a successful business.

But what does running or managing a successful business *really* mean? Does it mean making lots of money, or does it mean creating jobs for lots of people? Or could it mean giving customers what they really want?

The answer to all of those questions is yes. Let's pick up on the word 'success'. What does that really mean? Put simply, success can only be achieved if it can be measured. If it can't be measured, how can you know if success has been achieved? You can't.

Success – or failure – depends on many supporting factors. You cannot achieve success without being able to say you have or have not done something well. It's all about results.

If we start with a very basic question – why do you want to be successful? – then we could be here forever trying to define something that is different for every individual with that ambition.

Instead, let's look at what you can do to have an effect on the achievement of success.

For starters, being successful depends on many things that might be beyond the direct control of any individual. Let's look now at what's happening in the marketplace, since that is where the crux of the matter really lies.

For one thing, markets are becoming less stable because of various conditions. The economy fluctuates, technology is developing at mind-boggling speeds, customers are becoming more demanding and sure of what they want, and competition is becoming more and more fierce. The only thing we can rely upon here is that markets *will* change, and in order to make our businesses more successful, there is an ongoing need to be able to plan or adapt to that change very quickly.

1.2   THE NEED TO KNOW

Successful businesses, be they large, medium or small, all have one thing in common. *They need a plan.* Having a plan can mean the difference between success and failure. A plan is the key to success! 'Plan' is a small enough word, but let's define it:

> **Plan:** *to formulate or organise the method by which a thing is to be done.*

To my mind, this implies that those responsible for creating or managing a successful business must first know what it is they are formulating, what it is they are organising, and what is to be done. This is no small task! How many of us can really say that we know what we want, how we want it and what happens when we get it?

> **Consider:** *A competent driver would use a road map to get from A to B or from A to C via B.*

Everyone knows that, but so many new businesses set out without even the most basic of maps or routes. They embark on their journey with hopes and dreams and little else (not even checking the oil and water). They know what they would like to achieve, but they're not quite sure what to do and what the best way of doing it is.

Let's look more closely at this conundrum

First of all, successful management doesn't necessarily mean you need to have technical know-how of the intricacies of your business, nor does it necessarily mean you need to know every aspect of what your organisation does (although it can be useful!).

Success is easier to achieve if you know what you want to achieve and have a goal to aim for.

If you *don't* know what you want, then it will take longer to get what you want! Going back to the mapless driver, the road to success will be much longer, have more detours, and may experience head-on collisions as blind corners are taken in the mere hope of finding their journey's end. You need to know the limitations or boundaries that can stop or slow down that achievement. Without a map, how can you get to where you *want* to be? Without a plan, how can you know the best way to get *what* you want?

What can be done to increase the possibility of creating a successful business? Any advice at this stage could get very complicated if we refer to the thousands of texts that offer 'useful' tips on management styles and techniques. Instead, let's stick to three simple stages.

1. Identify your goals.
2. Achieve your goals.
3. Measure the success of those goals.

1.3   IDENTIFY YOUR GOALS

New businesses are very often the substance of dreams and desires. This might sound a little fanciful, but how else could the hopes for success, greater wealth and fulfilment be described?

Briefly turning away from the goals of business and looking at goals in life, many people buy a lottery ticket each week in the hope of getting rich quick and improving their lifestyle to match that of the rich and famous. That is their goal.

Let's not get too carried away with what is, for most of us, an unattainable dream or goal. Let's stick to being realistic here, and have business goals that are within our reach and where a realistic hope can become a realised goal, as opposed to a pure flight of fancy that can result in dashed hopes and expensive disasters, as many new and unprepared organisations often find out.

Achievable business goals tend to lean towards short, medium or long-term horizons. The short-term is almost instantly within grasp. Medium-term plans need some forethought and some degree of speculation as to what and how they want to develop. Long-term goals need to be developed beyond the realms of fantasy and wish lists into a vision that can realistically be worked towards by everyone involved.

$$Vision = Goals$$

Let's look at that equation in a little more detail

It is possible to have a *goal* without a *vision*. It is also possible to have a *vision* without a *goal*. For example, to be rich might be a person's goal, but they might not have any idea of how they might become rich – thus, they lack vision. Or they might have a dream (or vision) to enjoy life to the full, but have no specific thoughts as to what that actually means – therefore, they have no goals in life.

If we use the 'vision equals goals' equation in business terms, an example of having goals without vision might be to improve the profits by x per cent, but without any clear idea of where savings might be made to increase profits. As another example, someone with a vision but no goals may want to be the best in any particular technological field, but has no clear or well defined targets to achieve that level of success.

Wouldn't it all be more satisfying if we knew what or where we wanted to be or to do and how we could achieve it, instead of working aimlessly and not really knowing why we were doing what we were doing? This might sound very confusing – it's meant to! Without a vision or goals everything we do, whether in life or in business, can be confusing and unclear.

Admittedly, some degree of spontaneity might be lost with all this planning and forethought taking place, but spontaneity is a fairly unrealistic concept in the world of business. Spontaneity in business can equal a reactive response to unexpected changes – an approach that can leave an organisation struggling to succeed.

Let's look at some examples of vision and goals from a business perspective

Goals

- To be profitable.
- To increase the range of products or services.
- To be better than your competitors.
- To be the first.

Now let's look at how we can achieve those goals through basic vision statements.

Vision

- To develop a business that is financially successful and continues to grow and become more profitable.
- To create a working environment that encourages creativity and new ideas that help increase the number of profitable products or services in ten years time.

- To develop a product or service that is more successful than the competition through a skilled and trained workforce that can keep up to date with new technology.
- To be able to anticipate what the customers want and know that the skills within the organisation are capable of delivering new products before others.

At this stage it is enough to have a general idea of what your goals *might be* – they are something to aim for. This might just be an outline of a goal, an idea that sparks off enthusiasm to try and make something work, or something that motivates or enthuses others to help make things work. Nevertheless, they are goals!

The journey to success has started. You have an idea and you have a goal – now you need that map we talked about earlier to help you plan your destination and achieve your goals.

1.4 ACHIEVING YOUR GOALS

✓ You have a plan.

✓ You know where you want to get to.

✓ You think you know how to get there!

Business planning is all about achieving goals. It's also about recognising the obstacles that may get in the way of those goals, and it's about minimising the impact those obstacles will have on operational success.

Obstacles

What do you think of when someone suggests you are sure to encounter obstacles in business?

Three areas that spring immediately to mind might be:

- lack of capital;
- competition;
- bureaucracy.

> **Obstacles can be overcome by a comprehensive and well thought-out business plan. For example:**
> - Banks are more likely to offer you a loan to increase your capital or fund problems if you have a well thought-out plan.
> - A business plan can include market research, thus giving some thought to what competition is out there or on the horizon (for example, increased competition due to technological advances).
> - Red tape and bureaucracy can be tackled head-on and reduced if you can provide appropriate documentation to show the powers that be (for example, the tax man or local authorities) that your business can be taken seriously.

To fully overcome all of these obstacles, and also any that haven't been mentioned, it is important that any would-be business person knows their business thoroughly. That means not only understanding the product or service they want to provide, but also the marketplace they wish to enter into.

Some thought is given to this in later chapters. For now, let's suppose you have a wonderful idea for a new business – which is the best way to start on the road to success!

However, it is not the only start. It would be unrealistic to think that having a good idea is all you need to join the ranks of the rich and famous! Yet before you are put off and your imagination is dampened, it is important that you are asking yourself some fundamental questions.

Q: What's out there?

Q: Who is my customer?

Q: Who are my competitors?

If those questions can be answered, either fully or partially, my guess is that you have your basic business plan and are on the right path to achieve the goals you have set yourself. If you cannot answer those questions, let's have a quick look at how you can.

What's out there?

This means knowing more about your customers and your competitors. It's also about knowing what the financial climate is and whether it is the right time to launch a new product or service. It is not enough to have a good product or service!

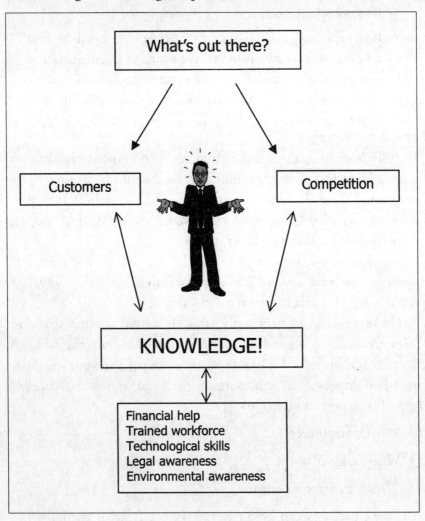

As with many businesses, start the sequence from the beginning.

- Start with as much financial help as possible.
- Develop a trained workforce that is able to make or deliver your product and service by developing their technological skills and awareness.
- Make sure you conduct your business within any legal requirements or government guidelines.
- Above all, have a good knowledge of the environment around you and the part your business plays in the overall scheme of things.

Who is my Customer?

Think this one through for a moment – it's not quite the straightforward question you might first think it is. Just exactly who is your customer? The person who buys your end product or service? Yes – but you have more than just those individuals as customers. For example:

- The company who provides the basic ingredients or components for your end product are your customers as well as your suppliers. If they do not deliver on time, then you cannot fulfil your order books on time. You need their expertise to complete your work.
- The individual member of staff whose skill is crucial to your success is also your customer, as they need to be employed to mutually acceptable standards or conditions of service (e.g. wages to match their skills or the kind of environment they work in).
- Your colleagues or staff could even be your customers! Their contribution to the organisation impacts the business as well.

In short, there are two kinds of customers: the customer who buys your goods or service, and the customer who provides you with the basic knowledge or skills to fulfil your targets.

Who are my Competitors?

Once again, this might also sound like rather a simple question. But do you really know who your competitors are? Have you looked recently? Today's businesses change so rapidly that it is reasonable to expect the competition to change just as quickly. So go on – take a look out there.

First, take a look at the same products or services that are available alongside yours. *Are* they the same? Or are they slightly different? What is it that makes customers choose between your product and your competitors'?

You *need* to know the difference if you are to maintain or improve your success. This can be done through a variety of means, such as market research or it can be achieved through monitoring the performance of your own product or service to see how and why it measures up to competition. Unless you know what it is your business is good (or bad) at, you cannot begin to be competitive.

Critical Success Factors

A half dozen *critical success factors* is the most you should list – if your business depends on too many factors, the business is unfocussed.

Examples of *critical success factors* for a transport organisation might be:

- Its customer base.
- The size of the transport fleet.
- Maintenance and repair facilities.
- Communications.
- Response times.

There you have it. Without those five *critical* factors, a transport organisation cannot operate successfully.

You might be tempted to add other factors such as cost of fuel, stock of spare parts, number of drivers or marketing and advertising. While these are important, they are not critical to success.

For example, a transport organisation can carry on its business without any one of these factors at any given time, or the organisation could find the resources for external suppliers instead of using its own.

Exercise

Think about what the *critical success factors* are that really and truly describe exactly what your business does. The key word here is 'critical'. Don't think about those areas of your business that are merely important. Critical success factors mean the difference between success and failure – not half-way measures. They will be the huge issues that affect your business. Keeping this concept in mind, make a list of your *critical success factors*.

_____

_____

_____

The gap between these two paragraphs has been kept deliberately small. That's because, in truth, your list *should* be small.

1.5 MEASURE THE SUCCESS OF THOSE GOALS

Some successes are easier to measure than others. For instance, it is easy to judge that a bank account is showing a healthy credit as a result of fantastic sales of widgets. However, it is less easy to show that a business is successful in selling knowledge and expertise (such as in design or computing skills). Although it is more difficult, it isn't impossible to measure success for such organisations. For instance, they might measure their reputation against their competitors by comparing how up to date their skills are, or how up to date their equipment is. What new designs are their competitors launching onto the market? Do they keep their key personnel, or are those valued employees moving across to the competition because it's a more successful company? If they do have a loyal workforce, what incentives or conditions do they offer that are better than their competitors? And so on.

Here are two questions that might be on your mind at this stage.

1. Is it important or necessary to actually *measure* success?
2. What does measuring success matter, so long as you are in profit or you feel you have enough business coming in to keep you going for now?

For a short-term project or operation, I would answer these questions by saying it isn't that important. Short-term payback is immediate and does not need to be measured – it either works or it doesn't.

As the old saying goes, success breeds success. This is certainly true some of the time, yet to keep improving and developing its performance, the successful company needs to steer clear of short-term complacency, and avoid sitting on its laurels in the expectation that everything in the garden will continue to be rosy just because it has a good product or a service that is currently in demand. Today's product or service could be tomorrow's fish and chip paper. Short-term thinking does little to guarantee successful performance.

To take that huge step towards long-term success and long-term security, at some point you need to be able to show exactly where it is that your success can actually be found. It may be in one particular function of the business, it may be one specific product or service or it may be the whole operation. Whichever it is, longer-term success will be out of reach until you are able to put your finger on the exact spot of success.

As success develops, it will become more and more important to be able to improve against any competition and increase your product or service knowledge.

Although there will be market or competitive forces that are beyond your control (such as a change in customer taste), you can do quite a lot to prepare your business for greater success just by recognising those things that you do well (your strengths), and by acknowledging those areas that are not so good (your weaknesses). Once you've recognised and acknowledged these areas, tell your customers and competitors! Feel good about blowing your own trumpet! Get smart at demonstrating how you can respond to the need to change your business if it's not quite right. Then, when you've become comfortable with that approach, measure the impact it has on your bottom line.

> *An easy way to do that would be to ask your customers what they think of your business. Do they like any changes you have made? Do they agree with you about your strengths and weaknesses?*

Some organisations are content just to know they are in profit (a short-term view). Some businesses are more complex and need to be able to adjust or to cut costs in different areas of the organisation if they are to continue to succeed.

Some businesses measure absolutely everything!

Activity-based Costing

Activity-based costing is a popular form of belt and braces accounting. It is a process that measures every component, every function and every part of the activity in producing the end product (or service). It is used to identify where overheads are incurred and where overheads or costs can be cut. A successful goal for such an organisation might be to identify where x per cent can be saved on the budget, whilst continuing to provide the same product or service. For example, if ten members of the workforce were employed to produce a product by hand, what would it cost to buy a machine that can replace nine of those ten staff? The machine may cost a lot of money, but in x number of years it will have paid for itself and saved the organisation that x per cent on the budget – or in other words, *successfully achieved its goal.* Yet, as with everything else, there is an opposite measure that should be taken into consideration in this particular example. Just to complicate matters, what impact will the machine that replaces nine out of ten staff have on an organisation if that organisation's continuing success is built on its reputation for hand-finished goods? I leave that thought with you!

Key Performance Indicators

Key performance indicators are another popular form of measurement. Organisations often need something that will provide a measure of how they are succeeding against competitors, or just against previous years' performances. For instance, when measuring the safety levels in particularly dangerous working environments (e.g. chemical waste disposal companies), how many accidents have there been this year compared to last year? In a hotel, how many bedrooms were empty during a normally busy week during last summer as opposed to this summer? Were there any other factors to be taken into account, such as whether it was a warm summer last year and a poor one this year, what your overheads were last year compared to this year, and so on.

Key performance indicators can be used to measure any aspect of an organisation's business. They need not focus on the tangible and clear-cut issues mentioned above. Instead, they could look at quality factors. For example, the hotel industry could look at the number of customer complaints or the number of maintenance jobs needed to keep rooms to a good standard. These performance indicators will inevitably go a long way in building a loyal customer base and will ensure the hotel has a good reputation, which in turn will bring in more guests.

We now know how to measure the success of our goals, but is it enough to know how to measure? Yes and no.

It's useful to measure, but not if those measures aren't used to actually achieve improvement. If they merely increase the workload with little sign of improving the bottom line, then why go through the process if it isn't of any benefit?

For now, suffice it to say that if measurement systems and procedures *are* used, they need to be used on a regular basis and as part of the overall way of working throughout the company if they are to prove useful in assessing where the company is doing well.

The quicker you can measure specific areas of success, the quicker you can respond to your customer's needs or to changes in the marketplace. To be unable to respond quickly to change will inevitably prove very expensive if an organisation has to wait for signals of impending financial disaster or suddenly realises that customers have taken their business elsewhere without knowing why.

By now I hope you agree with me that it *is* important to be able to measure success. You now know a plan is a good idea: it helps you establish and achieve your goals. Being able to measure exactly how or why you are successful is a useful way of building on those successes. Chapter 6 will explore *how* to measure success in a little more detail.

LET'S RECAP

✓ You're in business to succeed. You know it will probably be difficult to compete with others. You know that success can depend on knowing exactly what you want, and not entirely on what your competitors are doing.

✓ You know that a plan is crucial to pulling together all of your plans and dreams. Now you know your goals, how to achieve them and how to measure your success – but where do you want your business to go? Which direction do you want to take in order to make the best of your success?

✓ Times inevitably change, and that means that organisations have to keep up with changes as quickly as possible. To keep up with competitors or to move ahead of the chase, it is often necessary to be able to read signals from other areas of the marketplace and to know what is going on in the larger world of commerce.

✓ You know what you want to achieve and you have a pretty good idea of which direction to take to get what you want for your business. Yet the need to know what your customers want and whether you can give them what they want is of paramount importance. No matter how many goals you might have, they are nothing without customer knowledge and are irrelevant if someone else can deliver the goods or services more efficiently than you.

✓ All that information can be gained by measuring your success and by measuring what you actually do to gain those successes. Unless you understand everything you do and where you stand in the marketplace in relation to your competitors, your future plans will flounder at the first obstacle.

2

KNOW YOUR BUSINESS

Key learning points from this chapter are:
- The importance of understanding what is happening both within your organisation and in the external business environment.
- Where to seek the best help and advice to increase that understanding.
- The need to acknowledge the strengths and weaknesses within the organisation.
- The reasons for long-term business planning.

2.1 INTRODUCTION

As you read through this book you should be developing a systematic approach to working towards success. Step by step, we are developing a process that will enable you to gain confidence in recognising the whys and wherefores of being able to measure success within your organisation.

This chapter takes a look beyond the basic functions of your business (the products or services you provide, the technical processes you undertake in order to make those products or the day to day schedules you operate). It looks at the broader picture of the various functions happening around the organisation, both inside and outside of your business, and the way they can affect your hopes for success.

Some of these functions will be within your control (especially those internal to your organisation), but many will be outside of your control, particularly from external factors that dictate how you do business and how you can continue to do so.

Some functions, although initially beyond your control, can be dealt with in the way you *choose* to respond, especially once you have effective planning and measuring procedures in place. More of that later.

2.2   THE BUSINESS ENVIRONMENT

What do the words 'business environment' conjure up for you? You might be thinking of the wheeling and dealing of big business, with executive lunches and executive stress. Or you could be thinking of the economic climate. You might even be thinking of red tape and administrative issues.

All of those thoughts are correct, but let's look at the wider picture here. Let's examine internal and external environments and how they will affect the way you do business and the way they will help or hinder your success.

All organisations have internal and external business environments, whether they are commercial, public sector or voluntary. In the previous chapter, we looked briefly at 'what's out there'. This can include customers, competitors, financial institutions (such as banks), trade unions, suppliers, etc. Naturally, customers are vital to all businesses, and as such are given a vast amount of attention by those responsible for their business' success. Yet it would be unwise not to give other aspects of the business environment the same amount of attention.

Let's address that now.

2.3   THE EXTERNAL ENVIRONMENT

Without a doubt, if a business is to be successful it must change with the times, and to change with the times, it needs to know what is going on in the marketplace. A major key to success here is the speed at which organisations can change when necessary. Larger organisations might have their finger on the economic pulse and have a large number of staff dedicated to interpreting the changes that are occurring around them. But how many smaller organisations spend adequate time or money on examining the broader picture? I suspect not many. Too many are left high and dry and are unable to change quickly enough because they are caught unawares and have not recognised the need to respond to change until it is too late.

It is easy to become inward-looking, especially if business is ticking over quite nicely at the moment. But the way things are changing and the speed at which they are changing leaves very little place for complacency, or what I call the 'Ostrich Syndrome'. Burying your head in the sand of the marketplace achieves nothing more than sore eyes and obscured vision.

Since customer tastes change just as quickly as technology and product availability changes, it's not enough to rely on a good reputation to keep your place in the marketplace or to retain customer loyalty. You need to consider legislation changes, environmental constraints and labour market downturns or upturns. The external environment of any organisation never stays still.

The only thing you can be assured of is that it will change.

Since the 1960s and 1970s markets have gone global. Some might say that the 'customer is king', but in today's commercial minefield 'demand is king' – and supply has to keep up. That basically means that competition is fierce, and the only way to keep ahead is to be one step ahead (or preferably two!). It's an exhausting world we live in, in more ways than one.

If managers are doing the job they are paid for, they should be constantly looking at their organisation's external environment. They should be assessing whether any change in their business is needed and judging how they are competing with others. Getting back to the basis of this book, how can any manager make that assessment without some form of measurement by which to base those decisions? There are many ways of doing just that, and that is something we will look at later in Chapter 6.

Environmental Analysis

There's a fancy, technical-sounding phrase that sums up this continuous assessment – *an environmental analysis*.

It could be also be called 'looking at what's going on around you and seeing what the other person is doing'. In a business world dictated to by consumer fashions or tastes, businesses need to keep up to date with changing trends.

Even if your business is something that doesn't change too much despite ever-evolving technological advances (e.g. handmade cars, window cleaning, funeral undertaking, etc.), environmental analysis is something that needs to be done, otherwise success could well become failure.

Environmental analysis is relatively easy to do, especially with the vast amount of computer information and statistics now available from various sources (marketing information agencies, government, local authorities, libraries, Regional Development Agencies, etc).

There's also a lot you can find out without having to purchase any expensive data from professional sources. Below are a few key areas where information on your external environment can be found.

- Customer surveys.
- Supplier surveys.
- Business Link, Chambers of Commerce.
- Environmental groups.
- Banks.
- Internet.

Customer Surveys

Customer surveys are a very useful way of finding out what your customers really want. It is not enough to merely assume that what you are delivering is what they need. You need to be providing what your customers *do* want. To do that you could conduct a survey of all your key customers, but keep it short and sweet –

remember, they are busy people, too. Ask them simple questions, such as:

- Do we provide a good service (or product)?
- Does our product fully fit your needs?
- Do we deliver on time?
- Are there any areas where you feel we could make improvements?

Although this is a fairly simple process, there is a warning here should you want to pursue this kind of survey: you may get answers that you don't like! Be prepared for responses that don't exactly match up to what you think your customers think of you. If you are to undertake this kind of survey, be prepared to act on suggested improvements, because if you don't the whole exercise is a waste of time and money. Also bear in mind that if you ask your customers questions, you may raise their expectations, and if those expectations are not met, they may take their business elsewhere! Leaving those two potential problem areas aside, customer surveys are a very useful exercise and if you're in regular contact with your customers there shouldn't be too many surprises.

Supplier Surveys

As with customer surveys, keep supplier surveys short and simple. A few example questions are:

- Do we give you adequate notification of delivery dates?
- Are we efficient when receiving your goods?
- Are our requests clear and concise?
- Do any of our systems and procedures create unnecessary delays for you (e.g. payment of goods, production delays, etc.)?

Business Link, Chambers of Commerce, Local Authority Agencies

Business Link, Chambers of Commerce and other local authority agencies and economic development departments can provide valuable information on aspects of the business environment that are beyond your immediate reach or control. For example, they can help you with questions on legislation, the availability of funding, the economic climate in a very localised area, the availability of trained personnel, etc. These organisations can provide you with information that is local and up to date for your particular area.

Environmental Groups

Environmental groups are particularly useful to those organisations that have to work within legislative boundaries and win and maintain public support (e.g. waste disposal companies, engineering companies, etc.). An example of this that immediately springs to mind is the environmentalist campaign over Shell and the Brent Spar oil platform. Liasing with environmental organisations can save you a lot of time, a lot of money and win a lot of local support if their expertise is sought on any sensitive issues surrounding your operations. After all, you can't be expected to know every piece of legislation or to always be fully up to date on all political sensitivities in your area.

Banks

We have briefly touched on the support of banks already. Suffice it to say that without the support and help of financial institutions, operational success can be more difficult to achieve in the long run (or even in the short run!). Banks and the like will help you plan your business and help you think long-term as they, as much as you, want to see some returns for their investment and will be keen for you to succeed.

Internet

The Internet brings organisations immediately up to date. If you're computer-shy, there's sure to be some bright person nearby who is willing to get on the Web and look for useful bits of information for you. That information can focus on local markets, the national scene or even what's happening on the other side of the world. The global marketplace is shrinking rapidly, and if you don't keep abreast of those changes (be they in Huddersfield or Hong Kong) you cannot hope to have an organisation that meets customers' changing demands. You will just become a tiny fish in an evaporating puddle!

The amount of work needed to carry out an effective environmental analysis of what's happening around your organisation depends on the size and nature of your business. There is no defined way to do it, but by using the topics suggested above you should cover just about everything. If your organisation is particularly technologically based, more bespoke sources of advice and help may be needed. Whether yours is a unique organisation or a general service organisation, be selective with the sources of information you choose from as you could find yourself submerged in an unmanageable amount of data.

2.4 THE INTERNAL ENVIRONMENT

It is as important to understand the internal environment of your organisation as it is to understand its external environment. The internal environment is just as complex as the external one. Since all businesses are different, it is difficult to define a list of topics or functions that best describes the inner workings of every organisation, but let's give it a try. Immediate thoughts on key aspects of an organisation's internal environment might include any of the following:

- the size of the organisation;
- the number of staff;
- the number of products or services available;
- working conditions;
- salaries and hours of work;
- the management structure.

There are many more aspects you could focus on, and many would be common to whatever kind of business you are involved in.

How can understanding more about your internal business environment make you more successful?

> **Being successful = ?**
> It's easy to say you *want* to be successful.
> It's also easy to *say* you are successful.
> But can you explain *how* you are successful?

That's the answer to the puzzle – you can only be seen as successful if you can demonstrate or explain exactly how and why you are successful.

A proper understanding of your internal environment is vital, because that is where the difference between being good and being excellent lies. This is where you have some degree of control over how well your organisation does now and how well it can do in the future. Within your organisation you can identify exactly where things are going well or where there is need for improvement.

An efficient internal environment supports the goods, products or services that you supply. Without them, there is no business. If the administration, production lines, financial accounting or sales departments do not operate effectively, success will be harder to achieve. Thus, it makes sense to ensure that those functions within your internal environment are as streamlined and efficient as possible. It is even better to be able to say you have evaluated them all to see if and where you can do better.

In support of that, the following section is intended to increase the level of operational efficiency by identifying where your business is working well and any areas which are not achieving the standards you are expecting. Let's start with some basic analysis of what you do.

2.5 STRENGTHS AND WEAKNESSES

Your business' strengths should be developed continually and not taken for granted. Weaknesses should be acknowledged and understood rather than ignored in the hope that things will improve.

Do you know what your organisation's strengths and weaknesses are?

Exercise	
Strengths List what you consider to be the 5 greatest strengths of your organisation (or if you prefer, break it down to departmental level). 1. 2. 3. 4. 5.	*Weaknesses* Now list what you consider to be the 5 greatest weaknesses of your organisation (or department). 1. 2. 3. 4. 5.
Using the examples above, give what you believe to be the main reason(s) for those strengths. What do you think your organisation should do to develop these strengths to ensure further success?	Again, use the examples above and give an honest opinion as to why you think these are your weak areas. What do you think you or your organisation should do to strengthen these weaknesses?

The purpose of this exercise is to get you to recognise what your business does well. It is one thing to think you know, but it can be quite an eye opener when you put those thoughts down on paper. It is also thought-provoking to give reasons for good or bad performance. Again, this is something that most people think they know the answer to but may struggle with when trying to write it down.

If you are feeling brave or confident enough, why not ask others for their opinions on the strengths and weaknesses of your business? That will really give you a balanced picture of how good your business is. In other words, it will help you evaluate what you do from evidence gathered from colleagues or customers rather than on your own impressions.

I have no doubt whatsoever that your 'strengths' column will look much more interesting than the 'weaknesses' column and have more examples listed. Don't be fooled into thinking that lots of strengths mean that areas of weakness are minimal – that's doubtful! Everyone is comfortable in listing the things they do well, but it is more revealing to list those which you don't do so well!

Now that you have your list, what do you intend to do to maintain those areas you listed as strengths, and furthermore, what do you intend to do to make them even better? It's a tough question! It's much more difficult to improve on the good things than it is to recognise and improve your weaker areas. Weaknesses are usually more likely to be instantly recognisable and therefore easier to tackle. The slightest improvement can make a vast difference. Conversely, building on strengths takes much more imagination and perhaps greater courage to continue to develop and improve something that is already good.

Obviously, you shouldn't change things just for the sake of it. Change in the workplace can be unsettling or even traumatic for some. Unnecessary change merely serves to disrupt everything. Change should be positive, whether it is in rectifying weaknesses or in improving the scope for potential business opportunities. (Managing such change is discussed in more detail in Chapter 5)

For now, let's leave this section with a thought for the day:

> **Build on your strengths, work on your weaknesses.**

2.6 PLANNING YOUR SUCCESS

Now you've looked at what your organisation is good at and not so good at – so what? If you are achieving success at the moment, then well done! But are you really in a position to believe that this will continue?

If you have answered 'yes' to that question, you are either very fortunate or you have done your homework well.

If you have answered 'no', it could be because you either don't have any conviction that your product or service will continue for very long, or you have not given much (or any) thought to tomorrow, next week or next month. Or on a kinder note, you might be uncertain about the environment in which you operate (it might be very turbulent or very competitive).

Those of you in the 'no' camp may be suffering from 'short-term myopia' – running your business by gut feeling, by the seat of your pants, on a wing and a prayer or by rubbing your lucky rabbit's foot! In other words, more by good luck than by good judgement. Relying on past successes does not guarantee future success. How long can that luck continue? I hope you have at least asked yourself *that* question in an idle moment.

Going back to those who answered 'yes' just now – be warned, there's no time for complacency! What plans have you made to continue your success? Any? Some? A few? If you're confident about your short-term success in the next twelve months, how confident are you about being successful in the long-term, say in three to five years' time?

Again, these are not easy questions, but you do need to be thinking about what your answers might be.

Short-term Planning

Short-term plans focus on the immediate or urgent need for change. 'Short-term' covers anything up to six months or a year. It can mean just one day or it can be several weeks or months. Beyond a year, short-term becomes 'medium-term'.

Short-term planning is a very different kettle of fish compared to long-term planning. Short-term planning is *easier* than long-term, but both are equally necessary and equally important, since any sort of planning can only benefit you for the term it was designed for.

Some Reasons for Short-term Planning
- The need to fulfil a special order in a very short timescale.
- Quick-fix adjustments to bigger problems to get you by for a short while, e.g. high interest rates or the need to generate cash quickly.
- A change in working hours to cut costs to meet immediate financial problems.
- Pressure from outside to fulfil quick returns.

Some Abilities Needed for Short-term Planning
- You will need a quick grasp of the situation that requires changing.
- You need to be able to inform everyone involved as quickly as possible.
- You need to be able to monitor the situation on a frequent basis.
- You may need courage and creative thinking to get you through.

Some Problems with Short-term Planning
- Can be too reactive, with little thought given to the future.
- Can be unsettling for the workforce.

- Can give an untypical overview of the broader picture.
- Can be expensive, as knee-jerk reactions might eventually prove wrong.

Some Benefits of Short-term Planning
- Resources need not be tied up in any binding long-term plans.
- Commitment and motivation of workforce is easier to maintain.
- Any results (or failures) can be quickly identified.
- Objectives might be easier to achieve over a shorter timescale.

There is a place in any business for short-term planning, but that place is somewhat limited and is not a place from which to develop a sustained and successful business. If you are constantly reacting to changing needs or increased demand you will never be able to plan for long-term success. Short-term planning may fulfil an immediate need, but it can prove very expensive if you continue such an approach in the long-term.

2.7 LEARN TO PLAN LONG-TERM

I've deliberately skipped medium-term planning, as I think that is an area that is difficult to define. Medium-term planning can be anything from one year to three years to five years, but then again, long-term planning can be anything from three years to five years or longer. The overlap is fuzzy. When exactly does medium-term take over from short-term, and when does medium-term become long-term? It's difficult to say.

Let's concentrate here on long-term planning. If you find success and get through the short-term stage, you eventually move on to the long-term stage. That implies your business has survived beyond being reactive and is no longer at the mercy of customer trends or financial dictates.

It is very easy to plan short-term – you just need to react to a given situation. It's a different story to plan for the longer-term success of your business – it takes a large amount of skill and a

huge degree of commitment and determination to start and continue your plans. Some further thought is given to that commitment later in Chapter 4 when we look at ways to make the long-
term planning process work and achieve results.

As they say, what goes around comes around. For us, it's back
to the environmental analysis (discussed earlier), and understanding the marketplace as much as possible. Long-term planning can
almost be likened to a weather forecasting system – you can't say
for sure what will happen in the longer-term, but you can have a
very good idea about which way the wind is blowing!

Commitment to Success

In order to have any chance of long-term success, an organisation
must be committed to the long-term needs of the business, and to
the stakeholders and to the workforce who are responsible for
delivering that success.

It's almost an everyday occurrence to read of a company's
'commitment to its customers', as if that guarantees a quality
service with money back promises if not satisfied. All this sounds
good, but how does that commitment translate into the heart of
the company itself? For those companies that are brave enough to
promise 'quality' at all times, they must have full confidence in
the product or service they offer and they must have effective systems and procedures within the organisation on which they can
base that confidence.

Such confidence does not come from short-term plans. It can
only come from long-term visions, systems and procedures that
have been developed over a long period of time, ironing out any
problems or weaknesses as time goes on and more experience is
gained.

How can an Organisation Achieve this Confidence?

✓ Believe in the product or service you provide.

✓ Understand your business environment.

✓ Find out what your customers really want.

✓ Be prepared to change the way you work if necessary.

✓ Develop business systems that double check for quality.

✓ Accept only the best – be it supplies or personnel.

✓ Train your staff to excel at what they do.

✓ Only make promises you can keep.

A Long-term Future

You're now on your way to developing a commitment to the company's long-term future. You've studied what's out there in your company's external environment, you've had a look at what makes the company tick internally and you think your workforce is as committed to the future as you are – don't you?

Think hard. It's one thing to say, 'yes, we all want to succeed'. It's quite a different story to find a way to get everyone in the company thinking on the same wavelength and working for the same goals, and to fully understand the key factors that can influence your overall success or demise.

Does your company take the time to think long-term? This means everyone – you, the management team, the workforce and even the organisation's stakeholders.

You've developed systems that ensure a quality product, you know how to keep your customers satisfied and you have orders on the books several months ahead.

Yet the nitty gritty of long-term planning doesn't come with healthy order books (although let's not knock that idea – it's bread and butter to all organisations!).

> **Long-term planning means reading signals. It's like listening to a news programme on television or the radio. It's about understanding, or at least recognising, that your organisation can be affected by outside factors or incidents, and it's about not being caught on the back foot or being taken by surprise as the need for change arises.**

Some of you will say that that just comes with experience or you have gut feelings for such things. Some might say that it's difficult enough getting by from year to year without worrying beyond that. Sorry, but that's not good enough!

Instead of such complacency, and on behalf of your organisation's hoped-for success, you should be doing the following.

> **You must learn to read the marketplace.**
>
> **You must learn to anticipate.**
>
> **You must learn to think more laterally.**

Read the Marketplace

- Listen to what your customers and suppliers are saying.
- Find out why any customers are going elsewhere.
- Take notice of any new competitors and what their key strategies are.
- Know what your existing customers are up to.
- Keep abreast of the economic climate and make adjustments if necessary.
- Be ready for important technological changes.

Learn to Anticipate

- Avoid complacency – you can never be good enough.
- Never think you have done enough.
- Try to recognise early signals of change in customer tastes.
- Always acknowledge your competitors and try to keep one step ahead.

Think Laterally

- Think of new ways of working.
- Think beyond your basic products or services.
- Develop new lines that complement or enhance existing goods.
- Think of other services that you could deliver to your existing customers.
- Develop business partnerships to attract new customers.

Involve the Workforce

Your organisation's future depends on joint efforts. Your workforce must be involved and learn just as much as you about the need for long-term planning and thinking, and that means talking to them.

It is important to keep everyone informed at all times. Therefore, you need to develop an effective way of doing this that can be relied upon to give accurate, timely information.

How?

One very easy way of doing this is to set yourself targets and to measure or evaluate how you are performing against those targets. As well as knowing whether you are succeeding at what you do or are failing to hit the mark, an evaluation process helps you to make adjustments to those targets that *are* being missed or are recognised as being difficult to achieve.

In addition, regularly monitoring targets helps you to make any necessary adjustments *early* rather than later. That could mean the difference between making a profit or an expensive mistake!

> **Setting targets helps you monitor progress and measure success.**

For now, it is sufficient to say that setting targets and objectives is crucially important to any organisation, and this will be discussed in more detail later in this book.

LET'S RECAP

✓ The business environment of all companies is made up of the external and internal environments, each being complex and critical to success. Effort, time and commitment should be put into undertaking an environmental analysis in order to fully understand the impact other organisations and outside bodies might be having on your company.

✓ If they are to succeed and grow, all organisations should examine what they believe to be their key strengths and weaknesses. The need to develop strengths and acknowledge weaknesses is a vital part of the development process.

✓ Having identified those areas, it is then important to be able to view both the short and long-term direction of your organisation.

✓ Short-term planning addresses the urgent need for change, whilst long-term planning helps to develop the organisation's commitment to continued success and the achievement of established targets and objectives for the next few years. Both short and long-term planning need to be undertaken, as they complement each other in achieving success.

3

BUSINESS PLANNING

Key learning points from this chapter are:
- Understanding the need for a business plan.
- Guidelines for planning success in different kinds of organisations.
- The difference between strategic planning and operational planning.
- The importance of setting objectives for success.

3.1 INTRODUCTION

This chapter looks at the benefits of developing a business plan as a tool for measuring operational success.

Business plans are important to all organisations, be they of the commercial or non-commercial type, profit-led or public sector-based. All kinds of organisations need to understand what it is they are hoping to achieve and all need to be able to measure their success, albeit in different ways depending on which operational or marketing sector they operate in. Business plans are a very useful way of satisfying those needs.

Advice on structuring a business plan is suggested later in the next section, but for now we will concentrate on the thinking or methodology involved in developing your plan.

However, this chapter is not meant to give advice on how to write a *financial* plan, as that is a completely different concept to the sort of business plan we are concentrating on in this book. This might sound extraordinary for a book based on planning and measuring successful business performance, for what is success if not financial gain? There are other indicators that can be used to judge success, and this chapter goes beyond the financial

aspects of a plan and looks at the strategic and operational business planning issues that concern all successful organisations.

By now you should appreciate the importance of understanding your business and the need to measure how well you are
doing. Now you need to build on what you know.

- You know what you want to achieve.
- You know which direction you want to go.
- You have some idea of what might stop you from getting to
  where you want to go.
- You have lots of information to help you develop a successful
  business.

As with any other mammoth task, by now you have lots of information, but aren't sure where to start. Unfortunately, at this stage
you need to be a little less imaginative and a lot more task-
focused. You need to find a useful method to interpret the data
you have already collected. It is up to you to decide just how simple or complex your plan will be.

- It can be as simple as you like, or it can be as detailed as you
  feel you need.
- It can be scribbled on the back of a cigarette packet, or it can
  be a full-scale project plan with supporting financial spread-
  sheets and marketing analysis.

Whichever form you choose, you do need to decide what the best
way of *developing* the plan might be. You also need to bear in
mind who else will see and use the plan, such as the bank, the
board, staff, etc. Remember that your business plan is a business
tool, not just a document for information. The contents should
be used to plan what you want to achieve or change and to evaluate what has been done. You are now at the first stage of your
plan!

3.2 CREATING A PLAN FOR YOUR TYPE OF ORGANISATION

Whether you choose the cigarette packet or the project plan option will depend on the size of the task in front of you. It will also depend on the size of the business or on the size of your goals and ambitions.

The plan for a small or medium-sized business will naturally differ from that of the larger organisation. The advice presented here is being given to those who are concerned with the smaller end of the spectrum or who are just starting out in the business world.

Typical questions you might be asking yourself before beginning your plan may include:

• Who can help with finances?

• How do you know what red-tape is waiting to bog you down?

• Where can you get the best and most helpful advice?

Remember, even the most friendly local bank managers will definitely expect a business plan of some kind before they feel able to help you. Be fully prepared when attending that meeting.

Basic Tips on Seeking Financial Advice

The best advice is to keep things simple.
Find out what information the bank or financial adviser might need to know before you see them.
Make sure you provide them with answers, or at least be able to demonstrate that you know the basics of the business you want to undertake plus any difficulties you might foresee.
Know how much money you will need, what the overheads or costs will be, whether or not you need to purchase any equipment to make the business a success, where your income will come from and what the cash flow will look like.
Have some targets in mind, such as whether you need to employ staff now or in the future or how much profit/surplus you expect to make in one year, two years, etc.
And remember – you should have given some thought to what will happen if you miss those targets!

Basic Guidelines for Planning Success in Commercial Organisations

Guidelines here will depend on the structure of the commercial organisation. It could be entrepreneurial, a subsidiary of a larger group, a conglomerate or in partnership with others. Whatever kind of organisation, the commercial organisation's route for success will largely depend on its shareholders' demands.

The large-scale or commercial organisation may have sophisticated and formal planning systems that will complement its strategic direction, especially if they have been in existence for some time. Typical business planning concepts for such an organisation might include the following.

- Knowing the cost of the business.
- Understanding the company's competitive position.
- Recognising the direction the company wants to take.
- Defined strategic and operational targets.
- Ensured resources to meet targets.
- Understanding customer expectations.

These criteria should be used as a basis for the commercial organisation's business plan. An example plan might use the following headings as a framework.

1. Current financial position.
2. Key operational successes and achievements.
3. Competitive and environmental analyses.
4. Strategic and operational targets for the coming year.
5. Long-term plans (operational plans and the training and development of staff to fulfil those plans).

All of the above translate into fully understanding exactly what your customers want and knowing where you want the organisation to be in x number of years.

The level of competition is also something that needs to be studied constantly. New competitors or new products in your area of expertise will inevitably mean you have to change what you do. Exactly how much will need to be changed will depend on whether you are quick to respond or are taken by surprise.

This is where an environmental analysis pays dividends (as discussed earlier in Chapter 2).

Basic Guidelines for Planning Success in the Non-profit Organisation

Targets for the non-profit (or public or voluntary sector) organisations may focus on achieving operational objectives that are dictated by external forces, such as government funding, or on matched funding (where the organisation has to contribute an amount equal to that which they are given). In such cases, if an organisation does not achieve its targets, funding can be withheld or the organisation is given less the following year.

Although they are not measuring profit as the key success factor, non-profit organisations still need to develop some sort of system that will allow them to be able to say to their funding bodies that they are good at what they do, and therefore deserve to be granted aid or financial assistance.

If you are involved in the planning process in a non-profit organisation, you should be focusing on:

- the need to be clear about what is expected from you by any governing bodies;
- the need to be clear about what your business is;
- defined targets;
- the need to break huge targets down into manageable tasks;
- precise deadlines.

An example plan might include the following headings as a framework.

1. Current financial position.
2. Key operational successes and achievements.
3. Strategic and operational targets for the coming year.
4. Long-term plans.
5. Applications for future funding.

The focus here is about trying to maintain a clear vision or direction for your organisation. Without a hard, commercial focus there is a danger of wavering from predetermined goals and meandering haphazardly on what is hopefully the right business path. I am not suggesting that non-profit organisations are disorganised, rather that lack of focus is an easy trap to fall into for any organisation, particularly those in the service sector.

Historically speaking, publicly funded organisations are huge organisations. The trend today has reversed somewhat, with autonomous units being established within the larger parent department or governing body.

The systems and procedures that were adhered to in the past have in many cases been inherited by the public companies of the present day. This is also true for the work they undertake, with the need for financial and public accountability remaining at the forefront of any business planning procedure.

If things are planned properly, the mammoth tasks and operations of public companies need not prove unworkable. If things are not planned properly, deadlines will not be met, the service will not be delivered and funding bodies will not be happy. In that case, it is quite possible that success will be out of your reach, and funding withdrawn as a result.

3.3   LEVELS OF PLANNING

There are two distinct kinds of plans for all businesses, be they profit-led or public sector: the strategic plan and the operational plan. *Both* plans are needed by the successful organisation.

Definition

Question: What's the difference between 'strategic' planning and 'operational' planning?

Answer: Strategic plans need to get away from the daily grind of operational life and look outwards to the future, anticipating any changes that may effect the organisation in order to succeed. Such plans are aimed at securing the organisation's long-term direction.

Operational plans focus on the tasks and jobs that are required in order to complete *day to day* business.

That's the difference, albeit explained somewhat simplistically. So how do you begin your strategic plan?

Strategic Planning

First of all, it's important to list the different things that make up a strategy and which need a great deal of attention once you begin to plan.

A strategy is made up of:

- decisions on the organisation's future;
- the different pressures and influences that can make an organisation change;
- the ways an organisation chooses to respond to change;
- the ways in which different policies can be made to work together *successfully*.

Think holistically – don't just think about separate areas of the business and fit them neatly into the plan. Think about all of the key strands mentioned above and come up with a whole picture of where you want the business to go. Link the strands together to reinforce the core of the business.

All of the above criteria for developing a strategy require an organisation to examine what it does, by using the environmental analysis technique (see Chapter 2).

Without first looking at what's out there, it would be extremely difficult for any organisation to draw up an effective strategy. How can the future be planned for if you don't know the marketplace and other aspects of the environment?

Once an environmental analysis has been completed, take stock of what you already have and what you would like to have, and then try and understand the bit in the middle – the difference between definites and maybes.

Try this as a way of focusing on the gap.

Why do we need to develop the business?	What parts of the business do we need to change in order to be more successful?
Is there anything different we can do to extend the product or service range?	Are there enough resources to change the way we work?

By filling in these boxes, you should now be able to picture potential strategies that are important to the organisation's future success. It is always a useful tip to write things down, as it can help focus your thoughts and visualise the problem you are attempting to solve.

Rather than trying to develop lots of different strategic plans for the different areas of business, it might be best to first think bigger rather than small and local. For example, what is the most basic and fundamental change you need to make in the way you think about the business? If you have had a go at filling in the

boxes above, you may have formed some thoughts on this. Two
strategic examples are given below.

---

1. If you have identified a need for the organisation to be
   better at dealing with its customers, focus on that area as
   a core strategy, i.e.:

   **Develop a customer care policy that reduces the
   number of complaints and gives our customers what
   they really want.**

---

2. The need to invest in more up to date technology and
   equipment may be the main area of potential development, in which case a core strategy might be:

   **Reduce the cost of internal administration through
   modernised systems by investing x number of pounds
   in information technology and staff training by the
   year 2005.**

Strategies are concerned about the future of the organisation.
They do not get bogged down with the nitty gritty, day to day
operations that are needed to realise that future.

Operational Planning

You've looked at the bigger picture of what you want to achieve
strategically in order to be successful in your organisation's marketplace. Once you've decided on the direction the organisation
should take, focus your thoughts on that 'nitty gritty' stage.
You've broken down goals into manageable, and hopefully achievable, objectives. Now you need to really focus on *how* you will be
able to do it all. That takes us out of the 'strategic' planning stage
and into the 'operational' planning stage – the way to make plans
happen on the shop floor or in the operational departments.

Perhaps the simplest way of describing the difference between
strategic and operational planning is that strategies are decided
upon by senior managers, while the operational planning stage

tends to involve middle managers, whose role is to translate plans into actions, and the workforce who fulfil operational objectives. Those individuals are the ones who have to achieve success for the organisation at the operational stage.

It is reasonable to argue that since the workforce is responsible for successful operations at this point, it should be fully involved in the development of the operational plan.

In the spirit of keeping this advice simple, let's look at the key components of the operational planning stage. The key areas that effect operations might be:

• Finance.
• Customers.
• Suppliers.
• Workforce.
• Raw materials.
• Production times.
• Technology.

Of course, there may be many more areas depending on what business you are in. For now, though, let's use this list as a basis for the operational plan using the customer care strategy we looked at above as an example of turning a strategy into an operational plan.

First, let's ask some searching questions using the key operational areas above.

• What's the *financial* position at present, and what does it need to be?
• How can we give our *customers* what they want at a price they are prepared to pay?
• What can we do to get the best deal from our *suppliers?*
• What are the key issues concerning the *workforce?*
• How can we make the best use of the *raw materials?*

- How can we improve the *production times* and therefore save money?
- How can we make better use of *technology*?

By asking yourself tough questions at this stage, you will quickly form the basic framework of your operational plan. If you can identify the key factors that concern the operational areas, you will be able to keep asking more questions as the plan is developed. Never be afraid to ask yourself searching questions!

Past – Present – Future

If the operational plan you are working on is your first year's plan, you will need to focus on what you are doing and on what the organisation *hopes* to be doing by the end of the reporting year.

If this operational plan is a second or third plan, then you will be able to say what you are doing, what the organisation *has* done and what it *hopes* to be doing by the end of the next reporting year.

The operational plan needs to have some descriptive and supporting documentation of all of these facts, if only to make it more interesting to read. For example, you could include information on:

- Details of the achievement of specific tasks.
- How you have kept tasks on target.
- How you have monitored progress against the measurements taken.
- Comparison between last year's and this year's operations.

This stage of the plan is a chance to shout about those areas in which you have done well. It could also be an opportunity to explain why any targets have not been met, with suggestions on how areas could be improved upon. Use this opportunity to say what you feel needs to be said to those in a position to hear you to help improve business. However, don't use it as a negative soap-box – if there are problems, make sure you offer constructive solutions.

Once you've informed your reader of the organisation's current financial position and other key operational overviews, focus on something a little bit more defined – *objectives*.

What is a plan without objectives? It's like ambition without the courage to take a risk. Or it's like knitting without a pattern and just getting endless yards of a scarf! In short, it's practically useless.

Objectives are what make an operational plan manageable. They break down a programme of activity into workable pieces. Below is an example of what I mean.

Strategy:	To identify and develop a customer care policy.
Operation:	To undertake a customer analysis to find out what our customers really want.
Objectives:	1. Write a customer feedback questionnaire.
	2. Send questionnaire to key customers.
	3. Analyse responses.
	4. Identify key customer requirements.
	5. Build those requirements into a customer care policy.

Your customer analysis is very nearly complete – there's just one more thing you need to do: you need to set targets.

Using the example above, the targets could be proposed completion dates, percentages or numbers achieved by a particular time – whatever target is appropriate to the organisation. However, there is just one word of caution: make the targets realistic. There is little use in setting yourself a target that is beyond reach. It's not only a waste of time to pursue unrealistic targets, it's also expensive.

You've got your objectives. You've decided on your targets. Now what?

3.4   MEASURING AND EVALUATING SUCCESS

Setting targets without *measuring* or *evaluating* their success turns the whole process into a paper generating exercise. What use is that? Usefully measuring what you do and how you do it serves many purposes. For example:

- You can judge whether or not your business is successful.
- You can judge if individual products or services are successful.
- You can evaluate whether individual members of staff are performing well.
- Individual members of staff can evaluate how effective their managers are!

Measuring and evaluating targets should *not* be used or seen in a negative way. Targets should not be established just to hold individuals to account.

Instead, set targets for yourself and the organisation to provide the necessary yardstick from which to identify *why* the organisation is or isn't successful. From there you can prepare to change or enhance what you do. In other words, everyone should *gain* something from setting targets and reviewing their achievements.

> *Perhaps the most fundamental point is that objectives and targets should be agreed upon, and not imposed. They should be discussed and agreed upon by everyone who is involved in meeting the deadlines. How and when their objectives are to be reviewed should also be agreed upon by all concerned.*

Enough said about the minute details of targets. Let's look at a very simple example of how you might write up some useful targets for yourself or your organisation using the customer care strategy objectives mentioned in the last section.

Objective	Target(s)	Deadline
Write a customer feedback questionnaire	Draft questionnaire. Finalise questionnaire.	1 January 15 January
Send out questionnaire to key customers	Identify and list key customers. Send out questionnaires.	20 January 30 January
Analyse responses	Establish evaluation criteria to be used. Expect first management information data.	31 January 14 February
Identify key customer requirements	Submit recommendations to management.	25 February
Build those requirements into a customer care policy	Incorporate customer requirements (where possible) into a corporate customer care policy. Train staff to deliver those new standards. Send out customer care policy document to key customers.	1 March 1 April 1 May

As I said, this example is a very simple one. Your objectives and targets will most certainly be much more complex, but the concept is consistent whether the tasks are basic or complicated. It's the breaking down of the task into manageable pieces that is a key to success.

A key word for setting targets is 'flexibility'. You should be prepared to adapt to, but not to compromise on, any elements that are critical to business success.

If the business plan document is to be of use, you should try to work towards the targets you (or others) have set for yourself. In other words, they should be realistic and practical targets.

However, if you do not achieve them exactly on time, delays or change needn't be too disastrous. By breaking the task into stages and by consulting the document on a regular basis, you can quickly pick out those areas where delays are likely to occur or where you are ahead of deadlines.

What *would* be disastrous would be to think you are on target for the whole project and then suddenly realise, when it's almost too late, that one particular piece of the project is making everything else late or has been forgotten. A small, manageable problem will then become a huge one.

The beauty of having a plan containing detailed objectives and targets is that they break down the major tasks being worked on. By using a set of milestones to work towards, deadlines can be adjusted on a timely basis if need be. That way, there won't be too many nasty surprises.

LET'S RECAP

✓ This chapter establishes that business plans can be complex or simple – there is no set rule. Instead, much depends on the nature of the business and a sense of progressing towards success. The plan outlines the preferred way of working towards that success.

✓ We have looked at some basic tips for the smaller organisation in seeking financial advice to start up their business and we have looked at how to incorporate that advice into business plans for both commercial and non-profit organisations.

✓ Whatever the size of the organisation, a common theme of effective business planning is to have a clear understanding of what you want to achieve and the targets and objectives you need to set for yourself if the organisation is to have any chance of being successful.

4

EMBEDDING THE PROCESS

> **Key learning points from this chapter are:**
> * Understanding why it is important to find ways of making sure the new systems you have developed become accepted as normal working procedure.
> * How to find ways to get people involved in the planning process.
> * Recognising how embedding effective planning processes can benefit your organisation.
> * The importance of developing a good communications strategy to underpin success.

4.1 INTRODUCTION

'Embedding the process' is a slightly pompous way of describing a system that is accepted by everyone as a useful, effective process that's part of the day to day working routine. Pompous as it may sound, embedding the process can make the difference between long-term success and short-term failure.

The idea here is to show how important it is to have a basic understanding of why it is crucial to develop some sort of system for business planning and planning success if, at the end of the day, you want to see your business grow.

4.2 GETTING STARTED

To really begin this chapter let's start with some questions.

Q: Why do I need to embed the planning process?

Q: Do I need to continue to embed the process?

Q: Do I need to involve anyone else in the planning process?

Q: Wouldn't it be easier if I did it all by myself?

Those questions were trick questions! Here's why:

- If you *are* asking these questions, then you are *not* on the easiest path to business success.
- If you *are* asking these questions and *not* able to answer them, then you are most definitely looking to gain success *alone*. If that is the case, cut to the next chapter now!

If you're still reading this chapter, meaning you don't want to find success on your own and you do want others to help you, you should perhaps be asking the following types of questions.

Q: How can I involve everyone in the overall plan?

Q: How can I ensure that everyone gets a chance to contribute to the organisation's success?

Q: How can I ensure that everyone is involved at every stage of our development?

The difference in these two sets of questions is immense – it's the difference between working alone and without support (the first set of questions) as opposed to working as a team with everyone helping the business to succeed (the second set of questions). You will be able to take all of the glory if you go it alone, but you'll also be able to take all of the blame when things go wrong because you're over-stretched and unable to meet deadlines.

Conversely, a more team-orientated approach to planning can strengthen the success, bring success more quickly and most importantly, help create a positive atmosphere. More of that later.

Hundreds of books have been written on working in teams and the benefits this brings to companies. Cynics might well think that shouting about 'teamworking' as the sure way of achieving success is a fashionable management trend, such as total quality management techniques, quality circles, etc. But remember this – teamworking is not just the latest management technique aimed at helping management consultants and authors get rich; teamworking is all about knowing what each other is doing, knowing what needs to be done and working together to achieve a mutual goal – this, in short, is the planning process.

Let's get back to asking the sort of questions that are mentioned at the beginning of this chapter. My guess is that you'll quickly see how working as a team benefits all aspects of planning the business.

How Can I Involve Everyone in the Overall Plan?

The same rules apply whether you are developing a plan for a small, medium or even large company – involve *everyone* at every stage of the process. *Listen* to what the workforce is saying about the core of your business and the way the organisation operates. After all, they are the ones who know as much as you, if not more! They are the ones who can quickly identify problem areas or areas that can be developed or improved to increase the overall performance of their area of responsibility.

Perhaps the simplest way to involve everyone in the planning is to *ask* them to be involved! All of us want some sort of job security, if not for life, then certainly in large enough segments to be able to avoid undue stress. Part of that feeling of security comes from feeling valued and from knowing what's happening around us. To increase their comfort zones, individuals need to have as much information as possible. For example, they probably know in some detail what the organisation is actually making or selling, but does everyone know *why* their contribution is important?

- Do they know how fierce the competition is?
- Do they understand why there's a cost-cutting exercise about to be imposed?
- Do they know at which point in the production or selling process their contribution can actually make a difference and help ensure success?

If they do, then they are indeed involved in the organisation's plans; if they don't, then they are being left out.

How Can I Ensure that Everyone gets a Chance to Contribute to the Organisation's Success?

A simple approach at this stage will achieve wonders. Encourage an 'open door policy' – make yourself available to answer the questions that matter most to those asking the questions. Invite new ideas and constructive criticism rather than creating an atmosphere of intimidation or reluctance to voice new ideas or concerns. This will not only create a feeling of greater involvement, it will very likely develop a more creative approach to the future and to the development of the organisation.

Now we've arrived at the stage where we are open to new ideas and are not afraid to invite comments on the established way of doing things within the organisation. This is the right time for a word of advice: keep an open mind and keep your thoughts fairly receptive. Don't dismiss any off-the-wall ideas without some due thought. For every ten ideas, you may only get one absolutely fantastic idea that will pay dividends to your organisation, but I would argue that that's a good investment!

Let's consider what we have achieved by this stage:

- You have an open door policy which invites people to come along and talk to you.
- You are receptive to *all* ideas, both good and bad.
- You listen to what everyone is saying.

This all fosters an element of *trust* in the workplace, and what better start is there to a rosy future?

How Can I Ensure that Everyone is Involved at Every Stage of the Organisation's Development?

Communication is the key here. It is far better to over-communicate than to keep people in the dark, but take it one step at a time. Give the workforce a sincere commitment to good communication – and mean it! This includes bad news as well as the good. Make sure every division, section or team is informed of plans and progress and is updated on a regular basis. Make an active role as a listener a key part of your personal commitment to good communications. We've discussed above how you can encourage creative thinking through building trust, etc. Build on that by letting individual divisions, sections or teams take some responsibility for discussing progress and future plans with their colleagues from other divisions or teams (which also develops cross-organisational links).

Information on long-term plans is as important to everyone as the short-term, day to day operational issues. Furthermore, if things go wrong or adjustments are needed, make sure everyone knows why.

4.3 THE BENEFITS AND DRAWBACKS OF INVOLVING EVERYONE

Let's look now at what the benefits or problems might be when an organisation adopts a philosophy of encouraging everyone to feel involved.

Benefits

Here are just a few of the benefits of involving everyone in the planning process, making sure everyone is kept well informed at all stages of the process and letting everyone contribute to the process.

- The more everyone is included in the development of business plans, the more the workforce will believe in the end goal and help create an organisation or business that really knows what it's doing and why. Individuals will feel that they are integral to the organisation and that they have something positive to offer.

- Owning something, or just part of something, helps ensure greater care and commitment to success. Anyone who feels that their work is valued will also feel important to the process.

- If everyone knows what others are doing and why, it goes a long way to break down barriers or negative attitudes. Awareness of what colleagues do helps everyone to look at the bigger picture instead of narrowly focusing on their own particular area of work. There is no faster way to create bad feelings at work than to leave people in the dark on issues or decisions that may ultimately affect them. Bad feelings do little to help an organisation succeed.

- To give individuals the opportunity to play an active part in the day to day and long-term plans can encourage creative thinking in the workplace. Such opportunities could be small gestures, such as being invited to meetings or presentations or individuals could be asked for their opinion, knowing it will be considered or implemented and resulting in that very big word again – *trust*!

Drawbacks

We've looked at some of the benefits of encouraging others to become involved in the overall planning process. To reinforce the benefits of teamworking, it is revealing to look at the real problems of trying to plan and do everything on your own.

For those of you who seek to run things your own way, it is my guess that you will experience some of the following.

- Loss of control over the day to day management of the process as you try to do too much.
- Time wasted in unravelling confusion over the direction of the organisation as you frantically try to do and know absolutely everything, leaving others confused about what they are supposed to be doing.
- Imagine the added burden of increased costs as damage limitation becomes necessary when workloads become too heavy and you try to sort out the problems you have created.
- Your neck is on the block for bringing the organisation into a state of chaos.

In short, this is a recipe for disaster!

There aren't too many drawbacks mentioned here, but what massive drawbacks they are! You can almost feel a sense of panic and urgency just by reading that short list. Put in a nutshell, the drawbacks of *not* encouraging everyone to help at this stage will probably amount to an expensive exercise in power struggles and control as those who are uncomfortable with an open and productive approach to planning sink under their own self-esteem and self-worth. Isn't it much better to have helpful colleagues with mutual goals, all working in the same direction?

4.4 OWNING THE PLAN

What can be done to actually achieve this feeling of belonging and involvement in the business? Just take two simple steps!

> **First:** *if you do have tendencies to work alone, get away from your ivory tower. Let down the drawbridge and encourage and accept help from others.*
>
> **Second:** *using the latest management jargon, let everyone 'own the plan'. This applies not only to the end result — the glossy, beautifully bound final document — but from the very beginning of the planning process. Talk to people. Listen to people.*

No one should ask or tell anyone that they must 'own the plan' — that would be a sure-fire way to achieve exactly the opposite! Staff and colleagues would almost certainly become reluctant to play any active and supportive part in the business and instead do no more than the absolute minimum.

Another question to consider is how you can encourage this ownership. A few ideas are:

- Go slowly!
- Don't expect plans to be written overnight, at least not if you want a useful and realistic outcome.

- Begin by looking at one particular part of the business if that is more appropriate rather than trying to assess the entire range of products or services you provide. Keep it simple.
- Let someone else plan the planning! In other words, let someone else be responsible for some of the work. You don't need to be involved in every stage of the process.
- Make sure everyone knows what is happening.

The opposite of 'owning the plan' is not being interested in it, not wanting to be involved and so on. Such apathy will do very little to increase the organisation's bottom line or the performance of the business. Economically speaking, it makes much more sense to try to get any reluctant individuals interested and eager to be involved. If the organisation produces boring old widgets as opposed to a product or service that anyone would give their eye teeth to be involved in, then it will be more difficult to raise the interest and the participation levels of an otherwise reluctant workforce. You will need to find a way that works for you and your particular organisation. No one said it was easy, but it will result in a better working environment.

Sharing the Ownership

This is aimed at managers and the workforce and is meant in its broadest sense (not about actually owning the business in terms of stocks and shares). Perhaps it can best be summed up as owning *part* of the business. To reach that stage, the level of trust amongst the workforce needs to be very high if managers are to be successful in encouraging others to take responsibility for that part of the work they have shown they excel at.

Earlier in this chapter we've discussed the benefits of getting everyone involved in the planning process and we've looked at how this might be done. Additional benefits of allowing or encouraging others to pick up the challenge of ownership are:

- Sharing ideas can improve the overall comprehension of different parts of the business, which in turn can improve individuals' skills.

- Individuals or teams who feel responsible for a particular function can achieve more if they discuss their ideas with others and share the development of new ideas and skills. Such a workforce believes in the organisation, is keen to succeed and wants to play an important part in the organisation's future development.

Embedding the process brings added success and benefits to everyone, but we've not yet discussed the missing ingredient to assured success. Read on.

4.5 COMMUNICATING SUCCESS

Management experts shout about it and human resource officials praise it. The need for *good communications* is seen by many as being crucial to successful working practices and to creating an atmosphere that is open and trusting. Communication is undeniably important to a successful organisation.

We communicate so often that we take it for granted. Every day we read books, write letters and listen to friends and colleagues. Sometimes we communicate even when we're not conscious of doing it, such as through the impact our actions have on others. Let's stick to the easier and more understandable spoken and written word as our basis of understanding communication.

Effective and useful communications can mean the difference between success and failure, and let's assume that every organisation wants to succeed and perform better in order to build on that success. It must then follow that if success is helped along by good communication, a good communications system needs to be developed. This may seem like a matter of common sense, but good communications systems don't fall in place automatically as the organisation develops and people learn more about what they do.

How can an organisation or business make the best use of this basic resource and ensure that the planning process is effective? Can better communication be developed or should it be imposed? The answer to both of these questions is 'yes', but one is infinitely more desirable than the other.

'Imposed' communications come from the bosses at the top of the organisation. Such communications are generally perceived as 'being told what to do'. It might get things done, and sometimes it might even get things done more quickly, but it's not very good for *effective* communications. Effective communications work both ways, where individuals feel valued and able to discuss any concerns or make suggestions fairly freely.

Non-imposed and effective communications require a very different kind of communication process. It is a process that takes time to introduce, since 'developed' communications are allowed to grow and improve. Just as gardens grow or blossom with careful attention and a fondness for the work, effective communications work the same way.

In a recent survey I took part in, the most effective form of communication in the workforce was found to be 'chit chat'. Some might call it 'corridor talk', since that is where staff might chat as they meet and talk about things that are happening at a particular moment. Some might call it 'networking', a fashionable expression for discussing problems or issues with like-minded acquaintances who might be able to help you resolve any problems or issues you are having difficulty with.

Whichever way you interpret 'chit chat', if it means greater awareness about the organisation or the work being done, then it can only increase knowledge and understanding.

Having now acknowledged the importance of communications, be they formal or informal, written or spoken, it is equally important to be able to manage the communication process. How should this be done when seeking to embed your new planning process? Here are some possibilities.

4.6 DEVELOPING THE COMMUNICATION PROCESS

When trying to embed any new planning process using good communications, the management structure of the organisation will dictate the best kind of communication process possible in that environment. However, that is not to say that the structure of the organisation will dictate the most *preferable* type of communication process. For example, those organisations that are run from the top by a strong, charismatic, entrepreneurial manager might not be appropriate for a two-way communications process. If that is the structure you operate in, then it is important to develop a process that will help overcome as many barriers as possible within the given constraints. It would be foolish to try to establish something that is unrealistic and is doomed to fail right from the start.

But let's not be negative – let's imagine the organisation is structured in such a way that staff *can* talk freely to managers and managers *do* listen to staff.

Such a structure might be a team of senior managers who each have a small but discrete team of middle managers. They in turn might have complete responsibility for the success of their operations. Such a structure might look like this.

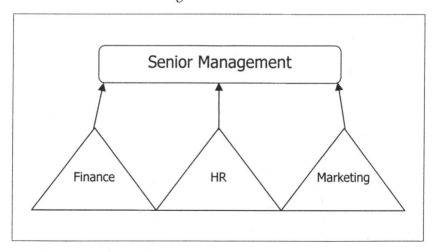

This type of structure might consist of a core of middle managers who work together on separate operational areas such as finance, human resources, operations or marketing. They might have complete responsibility for the day to day running of an organisation and only report to senior managers at specific times. Within those operational areas there may or may not be communication between the different areas.

In this scenario we have middle managers controlling their own areas and making many decisions on their own, but who have the appropriate communication channels to discuss any problems or ideas with those above them, i.e. upward communications to the senior managers. Sideways communications to other operational areas may also be possible when the need to discuss mutual work issues arises. However, the model is not complete. The missing link here is *people power*.

In our model, where is the means for individual members of staff – the workforce – to channel any of their ideas into an organisation's operational plans? No doubt the middle managers might pick up anything they think important enough to be pursued, and no doubt senior managers will listen to the middle managers that are passing on these snippets. Yet there is still a chance that this might not happen.

If you look at the diagram below, the middle managers' barrier looks difficult to get through.

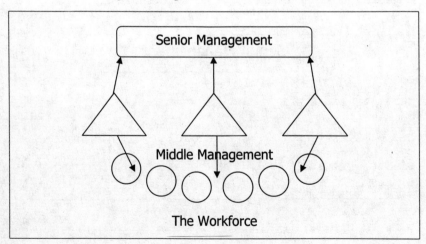

Wouldn't it better to instead develop a communication route that gives staff an opportunity to bypass the multiple layers of management to get their ideas or concerns heard? Consider this model as a suggestion.

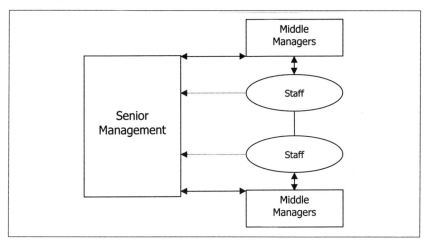

Let's look at the benefits of this model, where everyone can talk to each other.

- Staff can talk to middle managers.
- Middle managers can talk to both staff and senior managers.
- Staff can talk to colleagues in other operational areas.
- Staff has the opportunity to relate any ideas and talk to senior managers as part of the company's open door policy and communications strategy.

At this point you might be saying that it's all well and good to develop a fancy model or diagram, but how do you make it work?

In truth, that's for you to decide. You are the one who needs to figure out what best suits your particular organisation's style. All I can do is offer you a suggestion or two as to how you might usefully develop an effective, two-way communication process. For example:

- Have a regular agenda item at senior management meetings that allows the comments of staff to be relayed to the highest levels of the organisation via the middle managers. Senior management should then commit to answering their queries or concerns to the best of their ability, and they should do this promptly – that's crucial. Such a communications channel will serve a dual purpose. Not only will it allow comments from the shop floor to be heard, but it will also give the senior management team a better understanding of what concerns there may be amongst the workforce.

- Have regular information meetings that include *all* staff. If the workforce is a large one, hold several meetings within a short space of time – again, this point is crucial. Aim for a week, no more. If the meetings are spread over a larger period of time, a 'Chinese Whisper' syndrome might develop wherein one group is told one thing, but the next group might be told something that is just slightly different or said in a different way, which might then be taken back to colleagues and discussed slightly out of context.

- If the thought of holding regular meetings and putting the senior management team 'on parade' is not right for your organisation, the written word could be relied on instead. You could publish regular newsletters where staff are encouraged to submit questions for the management via the editor. This approach could give more anonymity to those who are uncomfortable with a more direct approach. The newsletter could be as glossy or basic as budgets allow – it is what is in it that matters.

Whichever communication route is chosen, you still need to bear one other thing in mind. While you work hard to find a method that encourages staff to communicate with the senior management, don't spoil all that good work by developing problems for your middle managers.

While the needs of the workforce are being met, it's very easy for middle managers to feel undermined or under-valued if staff are encouraged to by-pass them with their problems. This lack of management control will serve only to weaken the overall communication process, taking you back to square one.

If open communications are to be encouraged, it is important that *everyone* feels trusted and no one feels threatened (i.e. managers should not be held to blame if a member of their team raises an operational problem with senior management).

If 'closed' communications are to be avoided, you will need to find a way to ensure the communication process within your organisation is *seen* to be effective – as well as heard.

LET'S RECAP

✓ This chapter is meant to emphasise the need for everyone to be involved in the business planning and communication processes, and highlights the need to develop and encourage creative and useful discussions to which everyone can contribute. These discussions are the building blocks of the organisation.

✓ If an organisation is to succeed, it can't afford to miss any opportunity for grasping good ideas!

✓ Open and honest communications not only create a better management-workforce partnership, they also go a long way in developing a workforce that is keen to contribute as much as possible to a successful organisation. A creative workforce is much less expensive than any high power research and development programme or extensive marketing strategy – make the best of the resources you have.

5

THE HUMAN FACTOR

> Key learning points from this chapter are:
> - Understanding how people are the basis of any successful organisation.
> - The need to plan for your success from the bottom up, fully involving everyone within the organisation at all stages of the process.
> - The need to create an atmosphere that encourages good ideas and allows everyone to feel they play an important role in the organisation's success.
> - How to overcome any resistance to change through a clear commitment to your workforce.
> - The importance of encouraging everyone to think long-term if success is to be maintained.

5.1 INTRODUCTION

This chapter focuses on a common factor to all successful businesses, whatever sort of organisation you belong to, and that's people. Whether you are looking at large or small organisations, public sector or commercially-based businesses, the workforce (collectively or individually) is the main driver for operational success.

We have already briefly discussed in previous chapters how the workforce can and should be involved in the planning of success. Since people are what make things happen in businesses, it is worth reiterating the main 'people factors' touched upon earlier.

In Chapter 1 (*vision*), we suggested an organisation's vision might be to place the emphasis on creating a working environ-

ment that encourages creativity and new ideas that help increase
the number of profitable products or services in years to come.

Chapter 2 (*involvement*) looked at involving the workforce in
long-term planning to help organisations in their quest for success, and suggested that the workforce should be just as involved
as senior management in the need for long-term planning and
thinking.

Chapter 3 (*achievement*) highlighted the difference in strategic
and operational planning, using the 'people factor' to describe the
difference between strategic and operational planning. For example, strategies are achieved or fulfilled by the successful management of operational tasks. In turn, operational tasks are achieved
or fulfilled by the people within the organisation who translate
the strategies into achievable tasks. These fall under different levels of thinking and decision making, but work towards the same
goals.

Chapter 4 (*teamwork*) focused on 'embedding the planning
process', suggesting teamwork and a team-orientated approach to
planning as an effective way to maintain operational success. The
collective contribution of individual members of a team can
actively create a working environment that is positive and raring
to go!

So where does this bring us? Here in Chapter 5, all of the separate 'people factors' are brought together and looked at more
closely to further emphasise just how crucial this key resource is
to your overall business success. To achieve this, we will explore
how a culture for success can be developed and how it can be
maintained. What this chapter won't do is to look at human
resource management per se. There is no intention here to
explore HR management theories (e.g. appraisal systems, working
conditions, rewards, etc.).

Enough of what we're not going to look at. Instead, let's start
by establishing a basic framework for involving people in the
planning of success.

What springs to mind when you think of ways to involve people in your planning process?

- Informing everyone of what you want to achieve.
- Good communication at all stages of the process.
- A consultation process.
- Establishing shared goals.
- Encouraging creativity.
- Learning from your mistakes.
- Trust.

All are important factors, but can you prioritise them? I doubt it! None can stand alone – all need to fit alongside each other. There is no better analogy for planning success than a jigsaw puzzle, with people at the centre of everything. Take one part away and you'll never achieve anything that's worthwhile.

To start that jigsaw puzzle, it will be extremely useful if you have a picture on the box – this is not one of those terrible mind-bending exercises when you have hundreds of pieces and no idea what it looks like, as some jigsaw enthusiasts might prefer! Instead, let's begin with a modicum of sense and look at what you know (i.e. the picture on the jigsaw box):

- you know what you're *good* at;
- you know what you want to *achieve*;
- you know how you will be able to *tell the difference* between success and failure

You know all of this because previous chapters have explained how to find it all out!

5.2 BOTTOM-UP PLANNING

Now you have the picture on the jigsaw box – you know what you want to achieve and how you need to achieve it. You have all of the separate ingredients to success and you know the people you employ are the key to linking those ingredients together.

Bottom-up planning involves deciding the direction of the organisation through consultation with all employees, through open and honest communications and by involving the entire workforce at all stages of the planning process.

It takes the drivers for overall success away from the highest levels of management. It begins a process that emphasises the need for shop floor, operational knowledge and the way in which that knowledge is put to the best use in the pursuit of success. New initiatives and ideas (albeit ones decided upon by the powers that be) are left to middle managers and the workforce to interpret in order to find a working solution to make things happen and, of course, to achieve the best results.

Traditionally, management levels are very often viewed as triangular. The 'strategic apex' is the core decision-making focus of any organisation, where decisions about the organisation's future are made and dictated at the highest management level. Lines of authority go downwards to the workforce at the bottom of the pecking order (the broad base of the triangle). Instead, consider an upside-down triangle where the onus for success lies at the operational level.

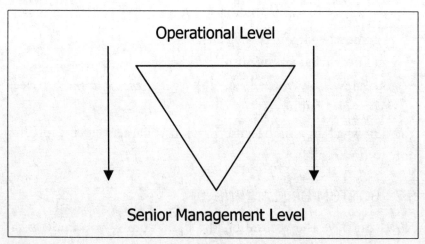

By turning the triangle upside-down, the workforce (or those at the operational level, including middle managers) are left to manage their targets in their own way as long as ultimate goals and objectives are met. In such a model, senior management is seen to be confident with this approach to business and is involved only at the monitoring and evaluation stage. The emphasis of the triangle has subsequently turned upside down, with the majority of the planning activity taking place at the operational level.

The beauty of this system is that the workforce and middle managers have agreed on the best way of fulfilling defined strategies. They have been clearly told what is needed and when it is needed by. They are given credit and trust for being able to manage the process as they see fit, with little interference from those at the top of the organisation (a 'hands off' approach to management).

Getting Started

Let's focus a little more on how to get started with the bottom-up planning process. Strategic objectives have already been defined and set at senior management level. It is vitally important that those objectives are communicated *consistently* to all levels of the workforce, including all levels of management and all members of the shop floor and technical and administrative support areas. Such consistency ensures that everyone hears the same message from senior management and everyone is aware of the direction their work will take (this was discussed in Chapter 4 under 'Communications'). Consistent communication means confusion and ambiguity is eliminated.

As a manager, your role is to make yourself fully aware of the areas that you are responsible for and to find the most appropriate way for your team to turn thoughts into actions. It's at this stage that you need to begin to formulate a plan specifically developed for your division or team, and that plan should be 'owned' and written by those who will be carrying it out. The divisional or team plan should then be used as a working document or tool, helping individuals and teams to plan their workloads, targets and priorities.

Strategic objectives that have been set by senior managers need to be turned into operational objectives that are achievable, measurable and useful to everyone in the organisation. The best people to do that are the people who carry out the tasks as part of their everyday work. Here's how to do it.

- Get your team together (preferably on more than one occasion).
- Make sure they understand what is being asked of them.
- Find out their views on those demands.
- Find a workable solution to any sticky problems (because there are sure to be some).
- Discuss and agree on reasonable targets that will meet set deadlines in good time.

Senior managers often ask for too much too soon. You and your team are probably the ones who have to live with those demands, so it's important to establish working solutions and the acceptance of set targets within your teams.

Such an approach to planning workloads and targets might sound like too much of a consultation process for some. There are those who prefer the 'do as I say' approach to management. There is little that can be said in support of such a management style in this particular book, for there would be little need to measure success in such an autocratic organisation. Instead, responsibility for success (and/or failure) would rest squarely on the shoulders of those dictating the business.

But let's forget such a destructive approach and instead imagine that you have been set some strategic objectives. You and your team have fully discussed these and are fully committed to making them work at an operational level. What do you need to do to make sure that level of participation is maintained and developed on an ongoing basis to ensure set objectives and changed objectives continue to be met?

It all comes down to just one thing – creativity in the workplace! Creativity produces an environment of challenge, which in turn creates an environment that is fresh, flexible and one which is fit enough to meet most, if not all, of the demands thrown at it.

5.3   A CREATIVE CULTURE

In all honesty, a creative workforce does not appear overnight. It involves a huge amount of effort by everyone, a strong commitment to the needs of the organisation and, if need be, a willingness to change the way things have previously been done. Even with the best will in the world and the co-operation of everyone, a creative workforce can take a very long time to establish.

Of course, if your organisation is made up of a workforce of creative individuals, as in a marketing company or technically-based organisation (such as computer software), then you must be one step ahead of the rest in establishing a creative environment. Yet even those types of organisations may have to work hard at making their systems and procedures creative rather than relying on the strength of creative individuals to fulfil (in their own particular style) operational aims and objectives. What I'm really saying here is that creative individuals don't necessarily make creative organisations. Instead, you need to concentrate on developing a creative internal environment through flexible procedures that welcome new ways of doing things.

What do businesses need to concentrate on if creativity in the workplace is to be encouraged? Go back to our inverted triangle and bottom-up management style. Ask yourself – what is the knock-on effect of this upside down management style? How will it affect the culture of your organisation and encourage creativity? Four words spring to mind.

1. Ownership.
2. Trust.
3. Commitment.
4. Empowerment.

> *These four words can help you to achieve success – but how?*

A great deal of information is readily available nowadays about creating a culture within organisations that is productive and effective. You may need to proactively develop the culture surrounding you in order to increase your effectiveness and creativity. By keeping our four key words in mind, you will fast-forward new processes that are needed when changing the way you do things.

Once you have a workforce that takes *ownership* for what they do, are *committed* to the success of the organisation and are *trusted* and *empowered* to manage and develop their own operations, you will have developed a workforce that is as keen as you are to succeed.

By letting individuals take more control of what they have to do, you change the working environment from one of policing and top-down management to one of participation and involvement by *everyone,* with planning decisions being made at every level (back to the upside-down triangle style of management). Of course, there still has to be a certain amount of monitoring – targets need to be kept on target, so to speak, and an appropriate system to do that needs to be developed. So long as this monitoring is done positively, things should run smoothly. Don't quickly blame folks for doing things wrong or taking too long. Look at the reasons for the problems. Learn from any mistakes. If neccessary, do things differently next time.

Such an approach will pay dividends in creating a 'creative culture'. Organisations are complex, and often demand creative solutions to difficult problems in order to succeed. Therefore, the working environment needs to be flexible enough to encourage creative thinking. To do otherwise just means that people won't even attempt to help you get the best out of what you are doing, or they won't attempt to help you solve your problems.

The Consultation Process

Imagine you have commissioned a team of management consultants to help your organisation's performance. Once their report is finalised and sitting on your desk and they have taken their leave (along with their cheque), what do you do next? That report contains all the different systems and procedures that they recommend you should implement if you are to be successful (we're almost back to a box full of jigsaw pieces!).

It's all well and good to get this expensive advice on what to do, but once the consultants have moved on, where do you start improving the way your company performs? One thing is certain: you should start with some clear thoughts as to how you think you and your staff and workforce can put the recommended new initiatives into place. That's the real definition of 'the consultation process' – not just paying an outside organisation to come in and tell you what to do at huge expense!

Forget any attempts at secrecy or confidentiality. *Consulting* the workforce at all stages of any new procedure is crucial to successful planning. This might sound shocking to some and may break all the old rules about only telling folks what they need to know. The consultation process is all about treating people as equals, giving a commitment to listen to other points of view and trying to find either a compromise or working solution to any areas of conflict or difficulty.

If your workforce is large, you need to find a workable solution to ensure everyone is given equal opportunity to voice his or her thoughts. If your workforce is small, the process will be easier, but it may well be more uncomfortable as personalities may overtake objectivity. By that I mean that where there are only a few employees, the consultation process may not be as honest or as anonymous as the same process would be in a workforce of several hundred people who do not have personal or day to day contact with key individuals.

The only drawback I can see to this consultative approach is the amount of time needed to do the exercise properly. Consultations can sometimes be overly extensive, taking procrastination too far, and they can sometimes become confusing unless a clear statement of intent or direction is stressed at the very beginning of the process (confusion does little for success!).

To my mind, the consultation process is the very core of 'bottom-up planning' and it may well be an uncomfortable procedure at times. Any comfort zone will be considerably diminished if you have a workforce that feels unhappy with your new proposals and feels they are working in an environment of chaos as a result of not being kept fully informed of proposed changes. Dividends will be paid back to the business and the investment of time will be well spent when you have a workforce of individuals who know and understand what your intentions for the organisation are.

> *Mushrooms do well in the dark – successful businesses do not!*

You have developed a new method of planning for success and you have found a way to let everyone know about it. You have given them a chance to let you know what they think about it all and have listened to new ideas. But let's be realistic here – there will probably be some resistance to the changes you are intending to make. If there isn't, then there's no need to read the rest of this chapter and you can move on.

5.4   RESISTANCE TO CHANGE

Consider the following points.

- You want to change the way you work in order to increase your chances of success.
- The workforce will have to change the way they have worked for the last few years.
- You've consulted them on the changes and you've listened to their thoughts.
- Yet you *know* there will be some who can't or won't change the way they work.

Ask yourself what the changes really mean. Do they mean the difference between success and failure? If the answer is 'no', why are you bothering to change things? If it is 'yes', then you *must* find an appropriate way to convince those who are reluctant to change their working practices or notions of complacency that change is necessary.

Overcoming Resistance to Change

There are many ways to overcome resistance to change in the workplace. One key aid to that process is the ability to evaluate and measure success. This means being able to *prove* to those who are unhappy that any changes are beneficial and well worth the effort.

In Chapter 3 we briefly looked at how objectives and targets need to be set when using a business planning process. Setting targets can go quite some way in reducing the fear of or reluctance to change. However, those targets should be established in a *positive and constructive* way, through *agreed* standards where everyone concerned can benefit. For example:

- the organisation benefits by getting the job done effectively and on time;
- the individual who needs appropriate guidance and direction from which to focus their efforts benefits by being able to measure their effectiveness as a major contribution to the organisation's success.

But how does resistance to change impact on the overall success of the business?

Resistance to change could be said to be a waste of energy. Think about it – what happens when someone doesn't like something and makes no bones about their discontent to others? Discontent leads to disruption, which can result in a reduction of the level of quality of the service or product.

In Chapter 4 we discussed the importance of communication and how effective communications can help break down barriers or resistance to change. Keeping everyone informed of what you want to achieve, how you think you can achieve it and the benefits the results will have on both the business and the employees needs to be stressed again and again. This is important not only to those who have placed their own barriers between themselves and you but also to others. Even the most committed employee needs constant reassurance of being on the right path to success if that commitment is to be maintained.

Reverse the Resistance

Consider this commonplace scenario:

- The organisation needs to cut production times and increase output.
- The least effective way of making those changes and the surest way of increasing the workforce's reluctance to carry out the work in that way is to simply tell them what to do.
- By discussing the reasons for the changes, by discussing and agreeing on how results can be achieved and by setting workable targets, you should be in a better position to get to where you want to be.

Does this sound like mere common sense? Isn't it exactly how *you* would expect to be consulted in such a situation?

By establishing an effective business planning process, you can dispel those feelings of discontent, resistance and even fear (for that is what often creates resistance to change). By constantly maintaining the focus on the direction and success of the business and any subsequent need for change, you decrease the possibility of resistance and improve the commitment to shared goals.

It would be foolish to think that everyone will be happy and satisfied with everything within the workplace once a business planning process has been established. Of course they won't. There will always be occasions when someone doesn't like the way you do things, the way the process works or the way in which the process is managed. There will even be pockets of resistance from those who refuse to be positive about anything. Such individuals exist in every organisation.

In such a situation, those personnel giving cause for concern will inevitably feel isolated in their negativity, especially as time moves on and the business planning process becomes truly embedded. For those individuals all I can say is you have to move with the changes. Time and business waits for no one. Join the team. Contribute. Share your experience and skills. Don't work alone!

We've already looked at target and objective-setting as a means of driving the new business planning process forward, but how will individuals look upon those targets and objectives? Will they feel challenged or will they feel victimised? Will they feel that you are telling them that what they do isn't good enough? It's very easy to create a feeling of negativity unless you show a commitment to managing the change openly and honestly and acknowledge that change is easy for some but perhaps not for others.

Changes in working practices can be as unsettling as change in other areas of life. Some will welcome it as a breath of fresh air, but some will feel very uncomfortable and may be defensive. Management skills will need to be well polished and honed when change is initiated, for who do you focus your persuasive efforts on when selling the benefits of that change? Should you focus first on those who are raring to go and are an example to others or on those who need more persuasion, thus leaving others frustrated and champing at the bit? In this case, you will have to choose whatever suits you best. Either way will be a true test of your management skills!

What should you do now?

1. *Establish* what your organisation needs to achieve.
2. *Break down* the overall aims into operational tasks.
3. *Discuss* those tasks with the individuals concerned.
4. *Agree* on achievable targets.
5. *Agree* on deadlines.

6. *Trust* the workforce to do the work.

7. *Learn* from any mistakes that are made.

This will inevitably be time consuming, but it will be time very well spent!

5.5   KEEPING UP THE GOOD WORK

Of course, some objectives are bound to be more crucial to the business's success than others. Those critical to success or failure are non-negotiable. (Regrettably we're back to the 'do as I say' scenario at this point.) Yet even if something is non-negotiable, it doesn't necessarily mean there shouldn't be some consultation regarding the finer points of the reasoning behind the set objectives. There will undoubtedly be some room for flexibility here, such as how best to achieve targets within given constraints or how existing working practises might be modified to accommodate the change, etc.

Up to now in this chapter we have looked at how to involve everyone in the planning process and how to overcome resistance to change. By now you should be well on the way to achieving success in the way the organisation plans its targets.

But what's next?

> **Question:** How can you maintain what you have achieved?
>
> **Answer:**   Through continued consultation, monitoring and evaluation.

What can get in the way of the best laid plans? It's all well and good to embark on new and improved planning systems and processes, but what happens when individuals are under pressure to meet unrealistic deadlines or targets? In reality, planning goes out the window and chaos management comes flying in as a means of solving immediate problems.

Learn to Plan Long-term

It is at such times that it is even more important to have a really good planning process in place, especially one that has flexibility built into the underlying systems. No plan should be so rigid that emergencies can't be dealt with without them having a catastrophic effect on the rest of the workload.

To keep up the good work of the planning process you have established, you should plan for longer than the foreseeable future – think at least three years in advance. Of course, no one can possibly guess with complete accuracy where the business will be in three years time, but what *can* be done is to do a little bit (or even a lot if need be) of scenario building – build some 'what ifs?' into the planning process.

For example, your business might rely upon technological advances that keep your organisation at the cutting edge of its commercial sector. That advancement will also depend on the economic climate of the time, which in turn will reflect the level of spending power by consumers, etc.

If they are up to speed with what is happening in the marketplace, then without a doubt similar organisations will have placed some scenario building into their planning cycles, giving them the flexibility to adapt their products or services as need be.

For smaller organisations, keeping up the good work of established planning processes might mean they have to be a little restrained in their long-term vision, and more focused on core business and fulfilling key stakeholder demands within a medium to long-term horizon. It is still important, though, that they have some thought as to where they want to be in the future and some idea of what future demands might be for their product or service.

As we discussed earlier in Chapter 2, fully understanding your marketplace or external environment will play a large part in ensuring that your business is not caught on the back foot and slow to read signals of change. That level of awareness and knowledge about what your organisation does and how it does compared to others offers a huge degree of comfort – not complacency! Such comfort works wonders in helping you keep up the good work of successful business planning.

However, this chapter is about the 'human factor'. What should you do about keeping up the good work of planning with your staff? How can you ensure that what you have established is maintained by everyone, even when the pressure of work tempts you to revert to a more reactive style of management in order to get things done? In this case, objectives need to be clear, realistic and understood by everyone. Simply put, the planning systems, objectives and targets needs to be realistic, achievable and simple!

As a manager, you need to find ways that ensure that your staff understands those targets and understands the impact their contribution makes to your organisation's success.

That can only be achieved if they understand the *whole* process and not just those operations that directly affect them. After all, no single operational function can ensure overall success. If necessary, it might be your responsibility to find ways to ensure that that level of knowledge is cemented into the day to day running of the organisation.

Yes, this means that there's even more for you to do as a manager. But trust me! It is necessary if you are to effectively play your part in your organisation's success.

LET'S RECAP

This chapter has concentrated on pulling together key strands in successful business planning and on a major planning resource – people.

✓ Without a doubt, I would argue that successful business planning and the measuring of success must be 'bottom-up', with staff at the operational level being a driving force in establishing how strategies for their organisation's future can be fulfilled through an achievable programme of agreed targets.

✓ For those embarking on such a radical approach to managing their business, they will inevitably need to take a visionary (and perhaps courageous) approach to turning the more usual form of management style upside-down. No doubt it will take some time before those at the top of the organisation are comfortable with such a 'hands-off' approach to management.

✓ It would be unrealistic to expect middle managers and staff to immediately accept such changes, and instead they might offer some degree of resistance to a new management style. Again, the common strands throughout previous chapters of this book have been called upon in this chapter to offer guidance in overcoming that resistance with good communications and teamworking. Realistic and purposeful objectives are also cited as being crucial to successfully embedding new procedures at all levels of an organisation.

✓ Embedding new procedures is all about making them work and in making them become the accepted way of doing things. Long-term operational success comes from long-term *thinking* – if your organisation does little to encourage such a concept it will struggle to keep abreast of the changing markets.

✓ There is only one thing that's certain in today's organisations – change is inevitable. How an organisation reacts to that change will dictate whether it is still in business in years to come.

✓ Senior managers, middle managers, supervisors, team leaders, staff and the rest of the workforce all play their part in surviving those changes and in making an organisation successful. As such, organisations need to invest in that very special resource, the workforce. It will be money well spent!

6

MEASURING SUCCESS INDICATORS

> Key learning points from this chapter are:
> - Identification of exact areas of successful perform-
>   ance.
> - Establishing key performance indicators to measure
>   success.
> - The use of appropriate key performance indicators
>   to improve operational confidence.
> - Understanding why it is important to repeatedly
>   measure success if it is to be maintained and
>   improved upon.

6.1 INTRODUCTION

This chapter focuses on the most tangible aspect of all business planning processes – the ability to measure whether or not your organisation *is* successful. This chapter will also help you to develop performance indicators that you will be able to use to show *how* the organisation is successful.

Let's go way back to Chapter 1 of this book, where we asked 'Why plan?'. Hopefully, by the end of that chapter you agreed with me that an effective planning system is the only way to establish whether or not you have achieved the goals and targets you set yourself (or your organisation) in order to be successful.

Now we are looking at the penultimate stage of that process – the ability to be able to *measure* that success (the final stage is being able to evaluate success. This will be discussed in Chapter 7).

6.2 WHY MEASURE?

Many organisations do *not* measure whether or not they are successful. Some successful organisations do not measure anything other than whether they are in credit or debit at the end of the year. Do they really need to measure what they do in order to be successful? In today's (and tomorrow's) consumer age, I think they do! Taking measure of what is being undertaken, planned or achieved complements an organisation's product or service portfolio. Here's how:

1. Measuring how well you do = product knowledge.
2. Understanding your product and environment = confidence.
3. Having confidence in your product and customers = minimising the risk.

Let's look more closely at each of those three statements.

Measuring how well you do = Product Knowledge

Many organisations might stand on their soapboxes and shout that they are successful and that their products sell well – and many do just that. Yet how many organisations in today's global marketplace are able to sit back and relax and do nothing to ensure their success continues? *None*!

Organisations are always at the mercy of changing customer demands or changing technology. How can organisations ensure they keep up with those changes or provide a product or service that is better than their competitors'? There is really only one way, and that is to be able to evaluate each stage of what they do, know why it is or isn't successful and how it can be improved upon.

As an example, many organisations undertake a process of activity-based costing exercises, where absolutely every detail of the product is examined and costed. No stone (or process) is left unturned. It is time-consuming and complex, but if done properly it provides the organisation with accurate details of the costs of each aspect of the product (or service) and where margins can be improved. Such a measurement system (and this is just one of many) provides the organisation with a strong knowledge base from which to build on and develop its future success.

Understanding your Product and Environment = Confidence

For those organisations that have studied what they do and what is happening around them, the result brings an added confidence through greater knowledge of what they do and what they do well. Confidence breeds success – and even more confidence! Success makes an organisation feel good about itself, just as it does for those individuals within it. Confidence may come from being the best in any particular field or expertise, from being at the leading edge of design or technology or from being able to anticipate the need for change before change is even demanded.

What are the benefits of such new-found confidence? Unless the successful organisation gets completely complacent, the knock-on effect must surely be a feeling of being on the right track, at one with the commercial world or even of being in a position of power or in a situation where the world awaits that organisation's next commercial initiative, recognising it as a trend setter in any given marketplace.

An organisation that tastes success may also feel more confident at taking risks. No one is suggesting anything foolhardy here, but fortune often favours the brave! An organisation that knows what it does well and *how* it does it well is in a position to take *calculated* risks. This might sound like comic-hero stuff, and we may be getting a little carried away in our enthusiasm – but why not?

Having Confidence in your Product and Customer Tastes = Minimising the Risk

Imagine that your organisation measures how well it is doing in its key areas and business has expanded as a result of taking calculated risks or having confidence in the market place. What do you think are the major benefits of such a comfortable position? As well as increased profits, increased shareholder satisfaction, increased status in any particular economic field or even a happy workforce, there is something else an organisation in such a position can feel good about. Hard to imagine?

Keep imagining. Your organisation has a good product and many loyal customers, which means you can afford the luxury of trying to develop the product or service even more, taking it one huge step forward into new areas. You have that comfort zone – or safety net – of a well-established reputation.

Conversely, if your organisation is not so confident, you will probably feel reluctant or unable to allocate resources on future developments and reluctant to take any risk of upsetting the status quo.

If we're not careful here, the daydream could turn into a nightmare! An organisation suffering from lack of confidence might be so fearful of changing or improving what it does that it settles for playing safe, in which case it probably stagnates and ends up losing its position in the market.

Enough of that – you're reading this book to make your organisation more successful, not worse!

Let's focus on those organisations that *do* measure their success or better yet, let's look at your organisation for awhile.

In Chapter 1 we looked at the critical success factors that described exactly what your business does. Using those success factors now, explain *why* they are your success factors.

Exercise

Critical Success Factor	Why is this success factor so important to your organisation?

I've made it easy for you – you only have to give three examples (remember what I said in Chapter 1: 'critical' should mean just that. Your organisation's success will depend on a handful of success factors, not hundreds).

Now that you've thought about the importance of your three examples, let's go a step further.

Using the same three factors and examples, list *how* you know they are so vital to your organisation. Don't just say here that they bring money in or they are what your customers want – expand a little. Dig a little bit deeper and tell me how you know this success factor is critical to keep the money coming in or keeping your customers happy.

Now think of an example of the measurement you use to *prove* you are successful in a particular area.

Critical Success Factor	What measurements do you make/ take to prove you are successful in this area?

By now you should either a) have some good examples listed and be feeling rather good about yourself, or b) you will be struggling to complete this simple test.

- **If it's a), bravo!** You know your business and your organisation is equipped for success. It has probably assessed its critical success factors and has a range of very useful key performance indicators from which to base constructive performance evaluation of its main operational areas.

- **If it's b), fear not.** All is not lost. Although this might look as if your organisation doesn't recognise its critical success factors or doesn't understand why it's important to be aware of them, it doesn't mean it can't change that attitude right now. It only takes one person to start the process off, and as you're the one reading this, it looks like *it could be you!*

Earlier in Chapter 1, we briefly looked at key performance indicators and the importance of effective measurements to support an organisation's drive for success. Now let's look in more detail at some specific key performance indicators, together with how they can help your organisation develop and build on its successes.

6.3   KEY PERFORMANCE INDICATORS

Key performance indicators (or KPIs as we'll call them from now on) are an effective measurement tool for all types of organisations, be they private or public sector, or service, product or manufacturing-based organisations. They can be used to provide quantifiable measurements such as staff absences, sales figures, minimum acceptable standards in service delivery, etc.

Used effectively, KPIs can help to ensure continuous improvement and help identify factors that are critical to an organisation's future development. Used ineffectively, they can be time-consuming, unhelpful and a real waste of resources. Therefore, getting the balance right is very important.

As well as being an indicator of performance (an obvious statement, I know!) a KPI is a tool which can be used to judge not only your own organisation's performance, but also to compare your achievement to that of your competitors.

For example, they can be used to show how well the organisation has done, how badly it's have done or how one function can be compared with another. They can be analysed to identify areas of high cost or waste or they can be used as indisputable evidence when trying to secure more funds or a change in working practices. However, performance indicators can also be used by your customers to judge how well you deliver their goods!

This warning might sound as if you are handing over control and leaving the organisation very vulnerable to the dictates of others. I think that would only apply if the service or product you provide is not up to scratch and your organisation is somewhat reluctant to give a 100 per cent commitment to what it does. Then again, any organisation that does not provide a quality service or product would not embark on a programme of performance indicators and could therefore choose to ignore this warning.

There you have it. Performance indicators are really all about completing the drive for quality and success. If an organisation is not focused on providing a quality product, they won't even begin to think of being able to usefully measure their success.

There is a trendy tendency nowadays to use what many of today's organisations call 'global indicators' as they strive to be the best at what they do in the global or international marketplace. We often hear of the Rank Xeroxs or the Hewlett-Packards of the world whenever 'benchmarking' the best performance is discussed. Yet does that mean the concept of key performance indicators is something everyone should be using just because the multinational (or global) organisations are? I'm inclined to say no, not all of the time.

The measures those multinational organisations use or the standards they set themselves against might work very well for them. However, the small or medium sized-organisation or the up and coming entrepreneurial company shouldn't even begin to measure themselves against the Microsofts or Virgins of this world! If they did, they might be disappointed, as unrealistic expectations can so easily be crushed. It is far better for smaller organisations to take a realistic approach to their measurements of success instead of comparing themselves with the giants of industry. Instead of measuring against them they should just watch from afar and have ambitions to be one of the giants some-day.

Let's look at some comparisons to clarify this point.

Large, global, blue chip organisation with billions of dollars at its disposal.	Small to medium-sized, up and coming entrepreneurial organisation.
Has the best in world R&D programmes.	Has limited resources for R&D, with limited success as a result.
Is the best in the world at next day delivery prom-ises – anywhere in the world.	Has limited resources for appropriate technology and staffing.
Is the best in the world at just-in-time stock manage-ment, resulting in reduced overheads.	Has limited resources and expertise to anticipate demand.

I know this is an example of extremes, but I think it usefully dem-onstrates the point I am trying to make. It's like trying to com-pare apples with pears – while they may have things in common, an apple is still an apple and a pear is a pear! The message there-fore is to be realistic in the measures you set yourself and your organisation. They must relate to *what* the organisation does, and relate to *how* it does what it does. Measurements should only extend to comparable areas of similar organisations where the results will bring added benefit to what you do. Remember: always ask yourself what the benefit to the organisation of measuring any particular operation or function is. If you can't find an easy answer to that question, don't bother measuring it.

To illustrate this point, let's develop the example we used above.

Medium-sized organisation manufacturing *hand-made* cars for international market.	Medium-sized organisation manufacturing customised *machine-built* cars for international market.
Needs to measure exact customer requirements.	Needs to measure exact customer requirements.
Needs to measure costs of each part of the manufacturing process.	Needs to measure costs of each part of the manufacturing process.
Needs to measure the cost of training a skilled workforce.	Needs to measure the cost of training a skilled workforce.

Spot anything? These two organisations, both in their own particular (but similar) niche market, have exactly the same critical success factors. If they don't know what their customers want, how much it will cost to give customers that choice or have the skills within the organisation to manufacture those specialised goods, then the organisation will fail. In addition (and this is where the added value comes in), it would be very useful indeed for these two companies to measure against each other to find out who does what better and to emulate their successes.

To Measure or Not to Measure

At this point I can't stress enough that you should only be using those performance indictors which can provide *useful* information. It's very easy for someone to devise a list of key performance indicators, but each indicator should be critically examined in light of what the gathered information will yield to benefit the organisation.

To get the best from any list of proposed performance indicators you first need to ask yourself the following questions.

- How long will it take to gather the information?
- What will the information be used for?
- Why will the organisation benefit from this information?
- When will the information be used again?

If you can't answer any of the above questions satisfactorily for any individual performance indicator, then strike it from your list! If you can't answer any of them, then they must be irrelevant to what you do or what you need to be doing.

If you *can* answer those questions easily, you have at your fingertips the sort of performance indicators that can be used effectively to measure success year after year or to evaluate current performance with previous performance. This consistent audit is the secret to successful key performance indication.

Up to now we've looked at the general concept of KPIs and why they are useful, whatever the size of your organisation. Now let's look at some examples of KPIs and how you might make them work for your organisation.

Benchmarking

This growing phenomenon is all about comparing one organisation's key performance indicators with another (and usually similar) organisation. The ultimate purpose in this 'show me yours and I'll show you mine' game is to find the best organisation in a particular sector or in a particular product or service range.

Benchmarking is a valuable exercise when the playing field is a level one. It is not a level playing field when genuine data is unavailable. As with any other element of competitiveness, there will inevitably be areas within all organisations that will classed as confidential and therefore unavailable for scrutiny, and it is usually those areas that would prove to be the most interesting in any benchmarking exercise.

Let's assume that benchmarking data is available and is being used to honestly audit mutual performance indicators. Who benefits the most from this exercise? It must surely be the customer. The knock-on effect of benchmarking will result in an organisation that is in an advantageous position not only to keep the customers it already has, but to bring in new customers as well.

How does an organisation begin its benchmarking programme?

1. Begin with an important first step – ask yourself what you need to benchmark.

2. Then ask who you want to be benchmarked against.

3. Always bear in mind whether you want to be the best or just as good as the rest.

4. Remember to include your customers and ask them what they ideally would like from you.

5. Before you start benchmarking, consider how you will evaluate and use the data you have gathered.

6. Never lose sight of the fact that benchmarking data should work for the organisation and not just gather dust on some chief executive's desk!

In a nutshell, if done effectively, benchmarking should prove useful to your organisation and to your customers. It should raise your competitive profile and it should ensure customer loyalty, which all translates into success. If it's done ineffectively, it is a waste of resource.

Service Level Agreements

Service level agreements (SLAs) are a promise by the service provider to provide a minimum standard of service, which is established and delivered to customer requirements. The essence of SLAs is to balance what the customer wants and what the service provider is able to deliver, at a mutually agreeable cost. As a key performance indicator, SLAs help to manage service quality and help to identify potential shortfalls or the need to develop services further.

SLAs can be used in both public and private sector organisations – wherever a support service is provided to customers. They give a non-legal commitment to provide a consistent approach to what is often the intangible side of business, e.g. cleaning standards, delivery times, response times, quality of customer care, etc.

The service industry accounts for more and more of the commercial world. Catering outlets are just one example of where the quality of customer service is vital to success. The cost of services to any organisation are being increasingly questioned as more value for less money is increasingly demanded by the powers that be. Consequently, it is important that organisations delivering such services are able to clearly state exactly where costs are incurred and where profits are made.

SLAs break down services into clear tasks, which in turn are then easier to manage and easier to cost. Most importantly, the service provider and its customers are able to work together as partners, with clearly defined agreements and mutually achievable goals.

Operational and/or Financial Targets

Both benchmarking and service level agreements require a huge commitment by any organisation if they are to succeed. As KPIs, they are both time-consuming and somewhat bureaucratic. If your organisation is not in a position to give such a commitment to these KPIs, you can still make use of more day to day, manageable targets.

The trick here is to keep things simple. Look at what you do (your critical success factors, if you like) and break them down into measurable segments. For example:

- How many complaints have you received in the last twelve months?
- How many items were returned over the last twelve months?
- How many days of sickness have been taken over the last twelve months?
- How many call outs have missed the promised two-hour response time?

Once you have identified what you want to measure and recognised why you want to measure it, you will need to maintain consistency. If the data is to prove useful, it needs to be managed in the same way each year. That way, you can compare one year's targets or achievements with the previous year's and be able to say in no uncertain terms whether you have been successful and where you have been successful. Such data and statistics measure success. Without these systems, how can you identify those areas that are the most successful or those areas that need attention in order to improve success?

Key performance indicators are what you make them. Whatever your organisation wishes to evaluate as a measure of its success can be termed a KPI. They can be as simple or as complex as you wish, but they are only useful if they are made to work and help your organisation to be more successful. Never stop asking yourself, 'Will this data prove useful?'

6.4 MEASURE AND MEASURE AGAIN

We now come to an important stage in the drive for success. You have embarked on a programme of gathering KPIs, you have collected the data you wanted and you have used that data to make your organisation more successful or to beat your competition. Excellent!

Now what? Well, just as in life, things move on. All the effort and hard work you and your colleagues have put into gathering that valuable data will soon be out of date unless you strive to keep it up to date!

In essence, key performance indicators are targets, and targets need to be monitored at all crucial stages, not just looked at when deadlines or destinations are looming or just around the corner. Such an approach to KPIs of any sort may well result in a nasty surprise as you go full speed around that corner blindfolded!

In short, use your KPIs (and targets) at regular intervals to assess how well the organisation is doing and measure how well (or badly) it does as a matter of routine.

Let's use an example of a new (and very small) entrepreneurial company, desperately trying to make sense of what it does and where it needs to be in the near future. Imagine a company that has been in operation for a year, but knows it needs to make a decision about whether to continue trading or whether to call it a day and close up shop. This company has previously worked from day to day, or from order to order, in the hope that the business will grow and they will become successful. They have technical expertise, enthusiasm and confidence in their product, but they are still struggling to make a success of things.

In reality, they are faced with chaos! They have given little thought to *planning* their success. They must sit down and find some direction in what they are doing and where they would like to be in the future (this takes us back to Chapter 1 and the map we discussed).

As a simple example of what this organisation could usefully do, the following example suggests clearly measurable (and manageable) targets over the given timescale (six months is used here for brevity, with the process repeating itself on an ongoing basis).

January	Assess overheads for the year. Identify areas of necessary reinvestment (e.g. equipment). Work out targets for the year. Agree on a deadline for throwing in the towel if need be.
February (and ongoing)	Monthly monitoring of income.
March	Quarterly review of budgets and targets.

This model is a simple one, but simplicity is invariably a useful concept when trying to avoid chaos.

Going along with the timetable used above, KPI's need to be identified and measured at appropriate stages. This will help to underpin the overall process of measurement and evaluation. For example, the quarterly review of budgets will be influenced by whether the KPIs are good or bad at that stage. Regular reviews enable any necessary incremental adjustments.

In our example above, the cycle of measurement is completed at the six month stage, when financial evaluation will then be used to decide whether to discontinue business or (hopefully) to build on previous (and measured) success and to improve the business still further. Measurement just goes on and on!

Step 1: Measure.

Step 2: Continue on or change.

Step 3: Measure again.

LET'S RECAP

✓ This chapter has emphasised the importance of not only measuring what you do, but also of being able to pinpoint how your organisation is successful and where it could possibly improve its performance.

✓ To do this, it is necessary to establish a form of measurement (or key performance indicator) that is relevant and useful to you and your organisation. Your chosen form of measurement doesn't necessarily need to conform to those systems used by others. However, what it must do is to be of value to the organisation's future and overall success.

✓ Spending too much time and money on a form of measurement that is not useful is a meaningless waste of your resources.

✓ It is important to establish measurement systems that can provide comparable, consistent measurements that can be used from one year to the next as past, present and possibly future performance standards are evaluated or predicted and success is built upon.

7

ADDED VALUE

Key learning points from this chapter are:
- To be able to identify areas that provide added value to the organisation.
- The importance of minimising reactive problem-solving.
- Understanding why your organisation needs to be flexible in order to achieve success.
- How to continue success.

7.1 INTRODUCTION

Throughout this book we have looked at how to measure success for your organisation. This is done through four key functions.

1. Understanding the environment you work in.
2. Having a process that enables targets and objectives to be established.
3. Using the results of those targets and objectives to measure how well you have done.
4. Setting new goals to develop continuous success.

Having already looked at those functions in earlier chapters, the term 'to measure success in your business' should mean something much more comprehensive than you might have previously thought. Without a doubt, the ability to be able to measure what you do and to have the mechanisms to measure your success provides you and your organisation with the ability to think and plan long-term. In turn, that expanded knowledge provides 'added value' to the organisation.

| Knowledge + Creativity + Skill + Learning = Added Value |

Added value comes from many sources, and as an achievement it rarely stands alone. More often, added value is the result of complementary functions, all of which are connected and support one another. Added value means the difference between an organisation doing something adequately and doing something that achieves greater success (be it improved reputation, increased profits, improved staff morale or quicker service, to name just a few).

Added value doesn't necessarily mean throwing extra money or other resources at the business. That is most definitely *not* adding value to the organisation – that just increases costs in the long run. Nor does it mean raising prices to reap more profit; you may actually lose money doing that, as customers may take their business elsewhere.

The opposite of added value is undoubtedly wasted resources. It is therefore crucial that you limit that wastage by questioning the merits of all tasks or plans. Always ask yourself, 'Where's the added value in this?'

To better understand the concept of 'added value', let's look again at how *not* to add value to an organisation. After all, it's sometimes better to start by understanding what you do want by first deciding on what you don't want!

7.2   REACTIVE VERSUS PROACTIVE

To my mind, 'reactive versus proactive' conjures up an image of chaos and confusion. For example, imagine an organisation that finds itself *reacting* to problems or customer demands rather than being able to *plan* what it does and take the lead in developments. If this applies to your organisation, you will more than likely find yourself working within an environment that is reliant upon quick-fix solutions, suffering from knee-jerk reactions to surprises or trying to find immediate solutions to immediate problems. In such a scenario, you would inevitably find yourself trying to work in the turbulent environment of a reactive organisation.

But what happens if we turn the title around into 'proactive versus reactive'? That conjures up a completely different picture.

A proactive approach indicates:

- a degree of control over what you or your organisation does;
- a positive and workable approach to an anticipated goal;
- A level of awareness and confidence in the ability of your organisation as a result of a better understanding of the internal and external environments.

Such a level of understanding could be said to depict a calm and more controlled environment, which is something much more desirable than the 'headless chicken' scenario of the reactive approach to problem-solving or tasks.

Let's get back to some thoughtful analysis of this section heading. To start with, let me ask some questions regarding the style of management you find yourself dealing with on a daily basis.

Have a go at filling in the exercise below – and try and be honest. Taking a good hard look at how your organisation reacts to the unforeseen is the first step in changing from a reactive approach to a more proactive and productive form of management.

Problem	What would be your usual response?	Yes	No
The chief executive has decided it's a good time to change company policy on its major product.	Is this a complete surprise?		
	Did you anticipate this announcement and provide your chief executive with research information on which he based his decision?		
One of your key customers is experiencing difficulties and has cut their order with your company by 30 per cent.	Is this a complete surprise?		
	Have you been in discussions with this customer and been aware of their problems and begun to liaise with them to find a solution that will help both parties?		
The board of directors has pulled the plug on the latest marketing initiative in order to save money.	Is this a complete surprise?		
	Have you anticipated this as a result of management discussions and begun to make adjustments to solve the problem?		
Your major competitor has invested heavily in the latest technology and is moving ahead of the race and taking away your customers in droves!	Is this a complete surprise?		
	Have you studied your markets and have a plan in hand to get those customers back?		

If you answered 'yes' to the second question in each box, then congratulations, your organisation is proactive in its understanding of the needs and direction it should take and has anticipated change.

If you answered 'yes' to the first question in each box, your organisation is reacting to problems as they occur and taking everyone by surprise.

Admittedly, the examples used above are fairly extreme, but if this applies to you, don't feel too downhearted. Even the most successful organisations have to react to some situations, if not on a daily basis, then occasionally. It would be foolish to believe that the organisation that can predict, plan or pre-empt absolutely every bit of their operations and future strategies can ever exist!

Perhaps the key to developing a more proactive organisation is to *minimise* the number of occasions when reactive management is used or is considered necessary. Keep the reactive problem-solving approach for the smaller problems, because the bigger problems should not come as surprises. Does that sound like a strange thing to say?

To those who believe it does, I would argue that the bigger the problem is, the more you should know that it's coming your way. The bigger the problem is, the more background noise it will bring with it – rumbles from the wider marketplace, murmurs of discontent amongst your stakeholders or competitors, etc. Bigger problems are very rarely stealth-like in their approach.

A proactive organisation is more able to:

- establish its own schedules and timetables;
- be more creative in its research and development;
- be a market leader;
- feel confident in meeting its customer requirements;
- be quicker in recognising the need for change.

> *The better your organisation is at planning, the more proactive it can be.*

At the end of the day, does it really matter *when* you solve your problems, so long as they *are* solved? Of course it does! As we're talking here about 'added value', remember that reactive management is fairly likely to subtract value – in other words, it can cost your organisation money. Who said 'ignorance is bliss'? That's absolutely untrue for today's businesses. Ignorance is expensive!

The Proactive Organisation

knowledge + creativity + skill + learning = added value

Knowledge = anticipating changes in the environment.

Creativity = being able to solve problems to everyone's satisfaction.

Skill = having the ability to change.

Learning = being better at what you do as a result of change.

7.3   THE FLEXIBLE ORGANISATION

Ignorance (or in this context, lack of planning) often results in inflexible attitudes in the workplace. If an organisation is inflexible in its approach to business, it is more likely to fail than succeed. The successful organisation must be flexible enough to take the inevitability of change in it's stride. As we have discussed in earlier chapters, the only constant in today's organisation is change. That change can be minor or major, quick or slow. Whatever the pace, successfully managed change requires an organisation to be able to bend and change its operations and procedures if it is to survive and adapt.

A flexible organisation:

- reads the marketplace and is able to anticipate change;
- recognises the inevitability of change and develops procedures accordingly;
- identifies critical success factors and focuses on what really matters;

- keeps the workforce fully informed at all times;
- constantly monitors what it does and learns from its mistakes.

All of the above definitions have been discussed in earlier chapters, but at this point it might be useful to reiterate examples of areas of added value for each point.

Function	Added value function	Measure of success
Ability to change.	Minimises losses. Maximises potential. Confidence in product. Enhances reputation.	Maintains or improves position in marketplace.
Effective operations and procedures that allow for change.	Minimises wasted time. Minimises bureaucracy. Enables a creative approach to problems.	Quicker response times to changes.
Analysis of critical success factors.	Minimises confusion. Allows effective resource allocation.	Availability of relevant and critical data.
Fully informed workforce.	Maximises commitment. Maximises response times.	Empowerment. Ownership. Co-operation.
Monitoring and learning.	Continued improvements. Minimal disruptions. Fully understanding the product.	Ongoing improvements.

These are just a few examples. Of course, there are many more examples of added value in the flexible organisation. There is also another useful, simple way of judging how flexible your organisation is. Look again at the key strengths and major weaknesses within your organisation or your part of the organisation (you may have done this earlier in Chapter 2).

Your strengths will inevitably reflect your areas of greatest expertise, enthusiasm or effectiveness. It will probably come as no surprise that your weaker areas will pinpoint those functions that are poorly planned, ill-informed or inappropriate. Understanding and developing operational strengths will enable your organisation to be more flexible in what it does and what it's good at.

Mistakes can only be classed as weaknesses if they continue without any attempt to rectify them or learn from them and move onwards. The more willing an organisation is to learn from its mistakes, the more informed it becomes and is better able to increase its chances of success. To learn from a mistake is to develop. To develop is to grow. To grow is to continue.

Added value as a result of learning can also be achieved by looking outside the organisation's internal environment. By recognising how another organisation builds on its successes, particular aspects can be emulated or modified to suit any organisation's drive for success. Although commercial espionage is certainly not being encouraged here, a lot can be learned from other organisations (or competitors) who operate in a similar fashion or who have comparable areas to measure.

This takes us back once again to the importance of a thorough environmental analysis in the very early days of a new initiative or development. Any knowledge learned at that stage would undoubtedly prove useful in shaping an organisation's drive for success. That knowledge could also highlight areas to be avoided, thus adding value to your organisation by minimising expensive mistakes.

For those organisations that fail to gather valuable information or fail to learn from their mistakes, the guaranteed result will be inflexibility, not only in how they function, but also in how they fail to resolve their problems (since there will certainly be some).

In support of that statement, it is a timely moment to give a few examples of operational inflexibility – whatever the degree of rigour, all of the examples are detrimental to success.

Inflexibility is the result of:

- a lack of imagination in finding solutions to problems;
- a bureaucratic approach to decision-making;
- rigorous and constraining routines;
- a lack of training in and development of new techniques.

None of these factors will necessarily completely stop an organisation from succeeding, but they will certainly slow it down. Inflexibility can be summed up quite simply as the fear of change. For those organisations (or its individuals) who are reluctant to change, inflexibility will be found in all work areas. Whether it is in the way processes are carried out or in the attitudes of the workforce, inflexibility can easily be reversed by allaying fears, providing a commitment to any proposed changes or by providing everyone with the opportunity to contribute to planning and the decision-making process at some stage.

As a disclaimer for any cynics, the flexible organisation is not just about pandering to stakeholders, workforce whims, quality initiatives, etc. At the end of the (commercial) day, the flexible organisation saves itself money just by being able to keep on its toes and not being caught on a very expensive back foot when change comes along.

The Flexible Organisation

knowledge + creativity + skill + learning = added value

Knowledge = the ability to recognise the inevitability of change.

Creativity = maximised potential.

Skill = the ability to learn from change and improve.

Learning = greater awareness and faster response times.

7.4   CONTINUING SUCCESS

We have now arrived at the final stage of the 'measuring success' process. To be in a position to continue your organisation's success should now feel a little easier, since a little knowledge brings huge rewards – but alas, only through even more hard work!

Imagine again the small company we looked at in Chapter 6. It is still struggling to establish itself in its field, but it is making some progress. It has now given a lot of thought to planning and measuring on a regular basis. Its workload is more organised. It has a better idea of what its profit margins are. It has even done some fieldwork on its competitors. Now it thinks it knows where it wants its business to be in the longer term. Yet how it makes it to that long-term position is just one more problem for it.

This young and hopeful business has won itself several contracts for work that will keep it busy for several months, but it is still worrying about the future. How can it maintain this level of work? Does it have enough staff to do the work on schedule? Can it keep its customers satisfied and win further contracts?

If sheer hard work and enthusiasm were the key to continued success, this company would certainly continue for some time. However, as we all know, there's more to it than that.

Luck undoubtedly plays a large part in continued success for any organisation. Yet it is not the major part, as has already been mentioned in previous chapters.

Let's think back to some of the key factors for success explored throughout this book.

- Identify your goals.
- Plan for success.
- Understand your environment.
- Think long-term.
- Measure success.

These five themes are the major aspects of success in the business environment. If you drop any one of them, you will leave a huge gap in your chances for maintaining success. For our imaginary entrepreneurs mentioned above, they would do well to have all of the above themes in mind, not just at the beginning of their drive for success, but constantly. Whether we are talking about that fictitious organisation or your organisation, the same policy relates to the next cycle of your planning process.

- You may have achieved your original goals, *but you always need new ones!*
- You have a good plan, *but it needs to be continuously updated if new goals are to be achieved.*
- You've already looked at your environment and your competitors, *but do you still know what's happening out there? Have you looked recently?*
- You've taken measure of what you do and what needs to be improved, *but never stop measuring what you do!*
- You've done all of the above, *but the long-term catches up with you, so keep rolling your planning cycle forward each year.*

Planning should be ongoing, a never-ending cycle. Once established, your planning timetable will become seamless, with no natural start or finish point.

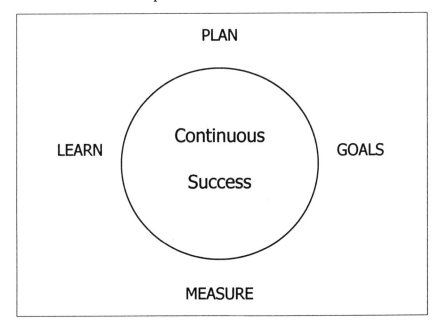

Continued success is not a magic trick that can be pulled out of a hat. It is more like sticking to the knitting, knowing what you do best and knowing absolutely everything that is useful to understand about the business environment in which your organisation operates.

For our entreprenerial organisation, their secret for success will probably lie in their attention to detail. 'Information, information, information' should be their mantra – or in other words, develop a long-term strategy. That strategy should focus on the future direction of the company, e.g.:

- What areas of their environment should they be taking advantage of?
- What areas of the business should they develop?
- What resources will be needed to develop in such a way?
- What can they do to be more efficient?

Coupling this list with the advice previously given in Chapter 6, our young company should now be a little more organised and a lot more hopeful of continuing their newly found success.

Lack of knowledge equals a lack of continued success.

The Continually Successful Organisation

knowledge + creativity + skill + learning = added value

Knowledge = the ability to expand or build on previous measures.

Creativity = the capacity to plan farther as a result of previous measures.

Skill = greater understanding of internal and external environments.

7.5 CONCLUSION

Having now reached the end of our final chapter and having explored many of the key themes of being successful, you will hopefully be feeling more confident in knowing how to measure your successes, are able to recognise the importance of finding ways to measure each aspect of what you do and have a better idea of how to build on what you do to achieve even greater success.

The depth of knowledge gained in those three steps will eventually bring added value to the way in which you manage or run your organisation (or small business). Always look for an opportunity to add value to what you do and always ask yourself where the added value *is* in what you do.

The absolute sure sign of success is added value. If you cannot measure how and where you are successful, you will find it very difficult (if not impossible) to identify the added value in what you and your organisation do.

Throughout this book we have explored how you can identify or achieve added value in what you do, and that is exactly what success really means. From the one-man entrepreneurial company to multinational organisations, success comes from having a germ of an idea and being able to make something of it, and being able to continue to maintain and improve upon that successful idea.

Those organisations that know what will make them successful and how to demonstrate their achievements have discovered the recipe for ongoing success.

If I ask you, 'Is your Organisation a Success?'

you should now be able to answer my next question,

'How is it successful?'